JENNIFER BAUMGARDNER is the publisher and executive director of the Feminist Press. She is coauthor of *Manifesta* and *Grassroots*, two best-selling contemporary feminist classics; and author of *Look Both Ways: Bisexual Politics*, *Abortion & Life*, and *F'em!: Goo Goo, Gaga, and Some Thoughts on Balls*. She has contributed essays and commentary to the *Nation*, the *New York* 's *All Things*

numerous a   schools acrc   at more tha

er has won
y taught in
e addresses
ast decade.

Originally from Fargo, North Dakota, Jennifer lives in New York.

MADELEINE M. KUNIN was the first woman governor of Vermont, and served as the deputy secretary of education and ambassador to Switzerland under President Bill Clinton. She is the author of three books: *Living a Political Life; Pearls, Politics and Power*; and *The New Feminist Agenda*. Currently a Marsh Professor-at-Large at the University of Vermont, she is a commentator on Vermont Public Radio and a blogger for the *Huffington Post*. She lives in Burlington, Vermont.

WE DO!

WE DO!

AMERICAN LEADERS
WHO BELIEVE IN MARRIAGE EQUALITY

EDITED BY

JENNIFER BAUMGARDNER
& GOVERNOR MADELEINE M. KUNIN

AKASHIC
BOOKS

Published by Akashic Books
©2013 by Jennifer Baumgardner and Madeleine M. Kunin

ISBN-13: 978-1-61775-187-5
Library of Congress Control Number: 2013938542

First printing

Harvey Milk and works of Harvey Milk are the property of the Milk Family and © & ® L. Stuart Milk. All proceeds from the use of the works of Harvey Milk are donated to the Harvey Milk Foundation. The Harvey Milk speech included in this volume is used by permission. To donate, go to http://milkfoundation.org/donate/.

Akashic Books
PO Box 1456
New York, NY 10009
info@akashicbooks.com
www.akashicbooks.com

ACKNOWLEDGMENTS

The editors wish to thank Alyssa Bowie, Devorah Shubowitz, Tyler Perkins, and Taryn Mann for their research and editorial assistance. Friendly expertise was also provided by staff at Freedom to Marry and Empire State Pride Agenda. Special thanks to Nicole Collins Bronzan, George Simpson, Erica Pelletreau, Representative Bill Lippert, Virginia Apuzzo, and Dean Hara. Last but not least, thanks to Johnny Temple and the whole Akashic Books enterprise for being an inspiring and righteous publisher, creating books that change consciousness.

TABLE OF CONTENTS

PART III: From Seeing Change to Sea Change

Editors' Note

Gay rights are the most significant civil rights battle of our time. The fight for marriage equality is the symbol of that battle. Barring same-sex couples from *the* institution that confers status, legitimacy, and visibility onto a couple or family is a final remaining prejudice, soon to be as incomprehensible as whites-only drinking fountains and women not being allowed to vote.

As recently as four years ago, in the 2008 election, supporting gay marriage when running for office was widely viewed as political suicide. A decade ago, it (along with abortion) was a reliable wedge issue deployed to undermine a progressive candidate's chance to win. And yet, certain brave leaders got there early, grasping the fundamental American values inherent in this battle, long before there was a groundswell of support for marriage equality or more than a fifth of our states having already adopted it.

The two of us come at the issue from different generations and from different roles within the political sphere—Jennifer as an activist; Madeleine as a former governor of Vermont—yet each of us has evolved dramatically in our perspectives. Jennifer, a third-wave feminist, has come to realize and respect the power of the institution, even as she remains critical of its historic patriarchal function. Madeleine, a second-wave politician, had to—within her political term—wrap her mind around the concept of gay marriage, even as she sensed instinctively that her only ethical option was to support it.

What role does gay marriage have in the larger movement for equality? Gay marriage is the first big monument of integration for this particular oppressed minority. Along with the abolition of slavery and a woman's right to vote, marriage equality will soon be the law of the land. Each of these historic paradigm shifts acknowledged a common truth: our shared humanity.

This isn't a book about the debate around gay marriage, how marriage should be defined, or whether being part of this institution is even something any self-respecting gay person should want. There is no attempt here to show "both sides" of the issue, nor is this book a comprehensive look at the speeches and political statements most important to the story of marriage equality. We don't tell the story of the countless grassroots activists or the brave couples who have made gay marriage not just a reality, but a human story with faces and lives with which we can identify and connect. Instead, this volume celebrates human rights by shining a light on some of the leaders who, when asked if they support gay rights in all ways, have eventually and enthusiastically answered, "We do!"

Initially, change was characterized by activists bringing lawsuits and then courts delivering decisions to a mixed-to-resistant public. Today, support courses through the electorate, magnetizing more and more people to see the essential fairness—the American-ness—of marriage equality. Whether or not progressives agree that marriage is of virtue, a critical mass of people believe that access to it is valuable.

In June 2013, the Supreme Court ruled that federal benefits such as a pension and Social Security must be extended to gay spouses (and that the 1996 Defense of Marriage Act was unconstitutional). Further, a second case decided on the same day found that the citizen-initiated amendment banning marriage in California (and deemed unconstitutional by lower courts) had no legal standing to appeal to the Supreme Court.

Because money needs to be where one's mouth is, 10 percent of the profits from the sale of this book will go to Freedom to Marry (freedomtomarry.org), to support their mission of winning same-sex marriage in all states and increasing the national majority in favor of marriage equality. Additionally, a donation will be made to the Harvey Milk Foundation to honor Milk's historic contribution to gay visibility, representation, and rights.

Jennifer Baumgardner & Madeleine M. Kunin, Editors
September 2013

INTRODUCTION
BY JENNIFER BAUMGARDNER

I'm a feminist and I've been once since approximately birth. My definition of feminism continues to evolve as my life unfolds, but at age ten I would have said it meant girls can do whatever boys can. Today, I'd add that feminism is a movement that makes it safe—inviting, even—to bring all parts of oneself into the room. The ability to be the whole of oneself is no small achievement in the face of daily opportunities to deny who we are and what has happened to us. But being one's whole self is the root of power, authenticity, and happiness. Feminism informs and intersects other human rights movements too, including the movement for gay rights. One of the most crucial gifts of that movement is that it enables all of us to consider, as feminism did, the institution of marriage and figure out whether and why it has value.

Feminists before my generation did heavy lifting when it came to transforming the role of marriage. Working women such as Helen Gurley Brown critiqued the notion that women had to be wed in order to be sexual and dispensed with the belief that a woman without a ring was either tragic or loose. Radical pioneers such as Laura X spoke out about violence and rape that, because it happened within marriage, was invisible and tacitly allowed, and created resources for women fleeing these injustices. Feminists such as Tish Sommers exposed the financial stakes when women were kept out of the paid labor force and vulnerable to being downsized via divorce from one's security as a housewife. And finally, feminists too numerous to mention redeemed and recast the single woman as desirable, adventurous, and independent while diminishing the social stigma of single parenthood. *Phew!*

All of this redefinition might account for why I never felt like I had to get married—or even that it was particularly smart to do so. In my twenties and early thirties, when I fell in love primarily with women, marriage was not only unappealing to me as a feminist, but also (poignantly) out of reach. I knew women who married other women in private ceremonies amid friends or who entered into domestic partnership agreements. Their bonds were legitimate and moving, but somehow "less than." After all, at that time there was no larger cultural understanding of gay marriage and no legal precedent. For me, being in a same-sex relationship removed the obligation and the opportunity of marriage. That loss was a little sad—I felt excluded; I wanted, in some way, the acceptance that being married equaled in my head. Not marrying my girlfriend could almost be a choice I made—except for the fact that the decision had been made for me by law and culture.

But then, at thirty-eight, I met Michael. At the time, I was a harried-but-happy single mother coparenting in an ersatz fashion with my son's father. Then, seemingly overnight, I was madly in love, pregnant with my second son, and headfirst into the chaos of blended family life. This relationship with Michael was different than what had come before—we wanted to make a family together. In fact, we hoped to take care of each other always. A few months after Magnus, our second child, was born, I realized that I wanted to marry Michael. It's hard to explain why—it was more a moment of intimacy between us that provoked it than anything conscious—but I had this instinct that I was safer and more myself with him than I had ever been before in a relationship, and that getting married would both indicate that distinction and reinforce it. We didn't get married because we thought it was good for the children—we thought it was good for *us*. To this day, I sense marriage's power and primary import exists separately from procreation. And yet, the legal and public agreement we made to figure out what it means to spend our life together with love and mutual care no doubt has positive ramifications for our children.

Walking to the restaurant where we were to be married on May 22, 2010, I thought for the first time what it means to say the lines about "forsaking all others for as long as we both shall live" in front of God and one's family. The magnitude of what I was solemnly promising bowled me over. The fact that there were witnesses who heard me make this promise helped tether us. Knowing people saw me make that vow is part of the strength of marriage. The automatic respect accorded to a relationship once it becomes a marriage (which always felt arbitrary and annoying to me in the past) suddenly fell around my shoulders like a strong, protective arm and I relaxed a bit into its comforts and security.

Three years into the institution, the contours of "marriage"—what it feels like for me to be connected legally to Michael—is both a site of struggle and a place of safety. When I'm anxious about a deadline, with kids who are both demanding I play UNO and deliver snacks, and Michael chooses that moment to ask me to scratch his back, my feminist beliefs (soul-saving though they are) don't help me out very much. In fact, they lead me to rolling my eyes and mouthing, *I'm going to kill you*, when his back is turned. But when I think about our marriage vows and consider that I made a commitment to care for Michael and to receive care from him, I actually feel some inspiration to sit down and scratch for a minute. Being led by my vows creates a path to bring more love and consideration into our household—and into the world.

I've written in the past about my childhood being steeped in feminism, simply because "the movement" was changing the world without my doing anything. My childhood took place in a radically changed atmosphere from that of my mother, full of freedoms that I took for granted because they were, in fact, my birthright.

As a forty-three-year-old woman, I live within a different (though related) active movement now. Nearly every day, hundreds of times each year, I march up and down Christopher Street, traversing Fifth Avenue (where I live) and Hudson Street (where my eight-year-old son attends school). Along the way, I intersect Gay Street and then peek longingly into Bien Cuit as I rush by. I pause for a second at the Stonewall Inn, just before Seventh Avenue, the site of the riots in 1969 that marked the debut of the gay protest movement. Of late, this historic gay bar displays a giant photo of President Obama in the window, along with a quote from his second inaugural address:

> We, the people, declare today that the most evident of truths—that all of us are created equal—is the star that guides us still; just as it guided our forebears through Seneca Falls, and Selma, and Stonewall . . .

I pass kids making out in front of the triangle-shaped Christopher Park that features life-size white-lacquered sculptures of two couples—the lesbians seated on a park bench; the gay male couple standing nearby, as if chatting amiably. Two blocks north is the old St. Vincent Hospital, ground zero during the early days of the AIDS epidemic.

In other words, my every day begins simply and organically, surrounded by gay rights history and signs of its profound recent successes. After drop-off, I often linger in front of a poster for a weekly prayer vigil for marriage equality at St. John's Lutheran Church. The following words are emblazoned on it: *Our work is not done until all enjoy the freedom we now have.* As a child in the 1970s and 1980s, I attended First Lutheran Church in Fargo, North Dakota. If prayers were offered for gay people, it was to help them live a straight life. Today, at least some Lutherans feel an urgent moral imperative to pray to extend marriage to gay couples.

We Do! tells a bit of the story of that sea change, largely from the perspective of political figures. Through these speeches, we glimpse the world politicians encountered in 1978 when AIDS was not yet part of our consciousness, nor was the idea of a diverse and out gay community of suburban dads alongside sex radicals (and all identities in between). We see how a few people speaking up, representing gay people in order to interrupt the stereotypes and hatred, begat an even more powerful movement. We see the slow evolution of power for gay people in the political sphere, as politicians sought their money and votes and eventually their counsel. Like many others, I rejoiced when Bill Clinton was elected in 1992 and was horrified when he signed on to "Don't Ask, Don't Tell" and the so-called Defense of Marriage Act. For many years, only a few leaders dared to state that gay relationships deserved the same rights as straight relationships. President Obama (another for whom progressives rejoiced) only recently came around on this after being nudged by his louder vice president. *We Do!* illustrates how, in the course of a single decade, activism around the institution of marriage—using the vocabulary of love and family—has transformed gay rights from wedge issue to civil rights success story.

Why has marriage become the signature issue of gay rights? Perhaps because, as lawyer/activist Evan Wolfson wrote in 1983, marriage is "an occasion to express their sense of self and their commitment to another human; a chance to establish and plan a life together, partaking of the security, benefits, and reinforcement society provides; and an opportunity to deepen themselves and touch immortality through sexuality, transcendence, and love."

Marriage, after all, is a way to protect a relationship enough so that you can bring all of the parts of yourself into the room. Ideally, you will be met and cared for by a person who is safe enough to do the same. This state of being gathers privileges from the government to support it: tax breaks, financial benefits starting with "two can live as cheaply as one," and, most profoundly, respect and legitimacy for the endeavor of caring for one another.

The institution of marriage is fraught. It has its archaic history as a way for a man to establish paternity of his children and manage property and inheritance. It contributes to the tyranny of coupledom. A marriage's dissolution still hurts women more than men. It's ironic that gay rights are gaining acceptance at the very same time women are losing some hard-fought victories, notably attacks on abortion and birth control. And yet . . .

The movement for marriage equality has helped this institution continue to evolve from a sexist, dynastic arrangement to a celebration of commitment between two equals. It takes seriously the radical words of the Declaration of Independence. Marriage equality demonstrates that our country is a living, always-growing entity of citizens still learning how to live up to the promise of "all [people] are created equal."

As Evan Wolfson has written, proponents of gay rights have death on our side: the demise of previous generations who mistook bigotry for piety and the passing of a time when you couldn't talk about gay love and relationships in polite company or with children. Walking along Christopher Street to school recently, past leather bars and St. John's Church, Skuli, my eight-year-old, asked me whether boys could marry boys. I said that we lived in New York State so, yes, they can. He asked me whether girls could marry girls and I said, "Yes, we can."

And if he asked me if I believe institutions can change for the better in a single generation, I'd look at the story of marriage and say, "I do."

Jennifer Baumgardner
New York City
September 2013

PART I

Becoming Visible

SUPERVISOR HARVEY MILK (1930–1978)

"The closet" doesn't just connote the shame of having to lie about one's identity and life. A closet is the small, dark, enclosed space where we keep things that we don't want to look at. Thus, coming out of the closet is more than truth-telling; it's entering the world and, with the act of being seen and reckoned with, changing society. After the Stonewall riots of 1969 debuted the rebellion against government-sponsored persecution, gay people were increasingly visible and becoming bolder. The next year, lesbians staged a zap at the Second Congress to Unite Women, wearing T-shirts emblazoned with the words *Lavender Menace* and signaling that lesbians wouldn't be in the closet for feminism. By 1973, the American Psychiatric Association announced the removal of homosexuality from the *Diagnostic and Statistical Manual of Mental Disorders* and began to promote antidiscrimination laws to protect LGBT Americans.

This was the world to which the first openly gay nonincumbent man to be elected to public office belonged, caught between exhilarating openness and high-stakes backlash. Long before there was debate about gay people in the military, Harvey Milk served honorably in the United States Navy on active duty during the Korean War. In 1972, Milk moved from New York to San Francisco and, with his boyfriend Scott Smith, opened a camera shop on Castro Street, an emerging gay neighborhood. Provoked by disgust over Watergate and buoyed by an exciting out gay community, Milk decided to run for office. Veterans of campaigns often say some version of "If you've run for office and lost only once, you haven't run for office." The trick to winning is to not be deterred by your loss from running again. By the time Milk won the race for San Francisco city supervisor in 1977, he had run three times.

The world of Harvey Milk was partly one of great change and freedom, as countless minorities—women, people with disabilities, people of color—began organizing for their human rights. Milk's tenure coincided not only with a movement steadily gaining momentum, but also with the beginnings of the organized anti-gay rights movement.

For instance, on January 18, 1977, Florida's Dade County Commission voted 5 to 3 to enact an ordinance banning discrimination against gays in employment, housing, and public accommodations. This was the first time a Southern city passed a gay rights law. That year alone, gay rights bills and ordinances were passed in more than forty cities and antidiscrimination bills emerged in twenty-eight state legislatures. The year 1977 looked as though it would usher in legal recourse to gays who were vulnerable to harm in every area of life and might end perpetrators' utter impunity. There was hope that cultural attitudes had shifted so that gay people could come out without fear of reprisal.

But 1977 also saw the rise of the organized backlash. A former Miss America runner-up, pop singer, born-again Christian, and Florida Citrus Commission's orange juice promoter Anita Bryant attended a revival at Miami's

Northside Baptist Church. The preacher there railed against the new Dade County ordinance that protected gay people against discrimination. Bryant established the group Save Our Children, attracting media outlets with her celebrity status and spreading her slogan, *Homosexuals cannot reproduce so they must recruit.* Vilifying gays as child molesters, rapists, and homosexual "recruiters," Bryant collected sixty-five thousand signatures, more than six times the amount needed, on petitions to repeal the law. Gay advocates and groups were not prepared for the political onslaught, intense organizing, and fear-mongering.

On June 7, 1977, known as Orange Tuesday, the ordinance was repealed by 69 percent of Dade County voters in a special ballot election. This defeat set off a wave of repeals of nondiscrimination ordinances in 1978 in St. Paul, Minnesota, Wichita, Kansas, and Eugene, Oregon. On the heels of these repeals, State Senator John Briggs sponsored Proposition 6 to ban homosexuals from teaching in public schools in California. The Briggs proposition ultimately failed, but some gay teachers and gay public officials still lost their jobs during this time of fomenting hatred. In the face of this bigotry, gay rights advocates gained strength and strategies. They protested Anita Bryant's appearances (including the very first "pie-ing" incident on live TV), forced her sponsors to retract their support through boycotts of any company even rumored to be promoting Save Our Children, and fervently boycotted all Bryant-endorsed products. By 1980, the Florida Citrus Commission did not renew Bryant's contract.

Harvey Milk didn't have a chance to savor Bryant's

eventual fall from grace. Less than a year after Supervisor Milk was elected, he and Mayor George Moscone were killed by former Board of Supervisors colleague Dan White. White served five years for the double murder, but Milk's tragic death—as his fame and influence were escalating—ensured his place in history. His brief career in public life marked the beginning of progay electoral politics. Milk demonstrated, in words and deeds, the power of having a "face" on an issue. Visibility is the first step toward liberation. Milk understood how even protest is a good sign for gay people, because it indicates that they are here, queer, and gaining ground.

The "Hope" speech which follows was Milk's stump speech, delivered often as he built his branch of the strong, gorgeous, and always-growing tree of human rights.

66 ## The "Hope" Speech[1] 99
Harvey Milk
July 24, 1977

My name is Harvey Milk and I'm here to recruit you. I've been saying this one for years. It's a political joke. I can't help it—I've got to tell it. I've never been able to talk to this many political people before, so if I tell you nothing else you may be able to go home laughing a bit.

This ocean liner was going across the ocean and it sank. And there was one little piece of wood floating

---

1. There are various transcriptions of this speech because he gave it in many venues. The version provided in this book is courtesy of the California Faith for Equality organization.

and three people swam to it and they realized only one person could hold onto it. So they had a little debate about who was the person. It so happened that the three people were the pope, the president, and Mayor Daley. The pope said he was the titular head of one of the greatest religions of the world and he was spiritual adviser to many, many millions, and he went on and pontificated and they thought it was a good argument. Then the president said he was leader of the largest and most powerful nation of the world. What takes place in this country affects the whole world, and they thought that was a good argument. And Mayor Daley said he was mayor of the backbone of the United States and what took place in Chicago affected the world, and what took place in the archdiocese of Chicago affected Catholicism. And they thought that was a good argument. So they did it the democratic way and voted. And Daley won, 7 to 2.

About six months ago, Anita Bryant in her speaking to God said that the drought in California was because of the gay people. On November 9, the day after I got elected, it started to rain. On the day I got sworn in, we walked to City Hall and it was kind of nice, and as soon as I said the word "I do," it started to rain again. It's been raining since then and the people of San Francisco figure the only way to stop it is to do a recall petition. That's the local joke.

But so much for that . . . Why are we here? Why are gay people here? And what's happening? What's happening to me is the antithesis of what you read about in the papers and what you hear about on the radio. You hear about and read about this movement to the right, that we must band together and fight back this movement to the right. The major media in this country has talked about the movement to the right so the legislators think that there is indeed a movement to the right and that the Congress and the legislators and the city councils will start to move to the right the way the major media want them. So they keep on talking about this move to the right. And I'm here to go ahead and say that what you hear and read is what they want you to think because it's not happening.

Let's look at 1977 and see if there was indeed a move to the right. In 1977, gay people had their rights taken away from them in Miami. But you must remember that in the week before Miami and the week after that, the word *homosexual* or *gay* appeared in every single newspaper in this nation in articles both pro and con; in every radio station, in every TV station, and in every household. For the first time in the history of the world, everybody was talking about it, good or bad. Unless you have dialogue, unless you open the walls of dialogue, you can never reach to change people's opinion. In those two weeks, more good and bad, but more about the words *homosexual* and *gay* was written than probably in the history of mankind. Once you have dialogue starting, you know you can break down prejudice. In 1977, we saw a dialogue start. In 1977, we saw a gay person elected in San Francisco. In 1977, we saw the state of Mississippi decriminalize marijuana. In 1977, we saw the convention of conventions in Houston. And I want to know where the movement to the right is happening.

What that is, is a record of what happened last year. What we must do is make sure that 1978 continues the movement that is really happening that the media don't want you to know about—and that is the movement to the left. It's up to the California Democratic Council to put the pressures on Sacramento, to break down the walls and the barriers so the movement to the left continues and progress continues in the nation. We have before us several issues on which we must speak out. Probably the most important issue outside the Briggs—which we will come to—is an issue on the ballot called Jarvis-Gann [which reduced property taxes and unfairly penalized those who don't own]. We hear the taxpayers talk about it on both sides. But what you don't hear is that it's probably the most racist issue on the ballot in a long time. In the city and county of San Francisco, if it passes and we indeed have to lay off people, who will they be? The last in, the first in—and who are the last in but the minorities? Jarvis-Gann is a racist issue. We must address that issue. We must not talk away from it. We must not allow them to talk about the money it's going to save, because look at who's going to save the money and who's going to get hurt.

We also have another issue that we've started on in some of the north counties, and I hope in some of the south counties it continues. In San Francisco elections we're asking—at least we hope to ask—that the US government put pressure on the closing of the South African consulate. That must happen. There is a major difference between an embassy in Washington, which is a diplomatic bureau, and a consulate in major cities. A consulate is there for one reason only—to promote business, economic gains, tourism, investment. And every time you have business going to South Africa, you're promoting an apartheid regime that's offensive.

In the city of San Francisco, if every one of 51 percent of that city were to go to South Africa, they would be treated as second-class citizens. That is an offense to the people of San Francisco and I hope all my colleagues up there will take every step we can to close down that consulate and hope that people in other parts of the state follow us in that lead. The battles must be started someplace and CDC is the greatest place to start the battles.

We are pressed for time so I'm going to cover just one more little point. That is to understand why it is important that gay people run for office and that gay people get elected. I know there are many people in this room who are running for central committee who are gay. I encourage you and there's a major reason why. If my non-gay friends and supporters in this room understand it, then they probably understand why I've run so often before I finally made it. You see, right now there's a controversy going on in this convention about the gay governor.[2] Is he speaking out enough? Is he strong enough for gay rights? There is controversy—and for us to say there is not would be foolish. Some people are satisfied and some people are not.

You see, there is a major difference—and it remains a vital difference—between a friend and a gay person. There is a vital difference between a friend in office and a gay person in office. Gay people have been slandered nationwide. We've been tarred and we've been brushed with the picture of pornography. In Dade County, we were accused of child molestation. It's not enough any-

---

2. *Milk is referring to Governor Jerry Brown, who took office after Governor Ronald Reagan and was more gay-friendly than his predecessor.*

more just to have friends represent us. No matter how good that friend may be.

The black community made up its mind to that a long time ago—that the myths against blacks can only be dispelled by electing black leaders, so the black community could be judged by the leaders and not by the myths or black criminals. The Spanish community must not be judged by Latin criminals or myths. The Asian community must not be judged by Asian criminals or myths. The Italian community must not be judged by the Mafia myths. And the time has come when the gay community not be judged by our criminals and myths.

Like every other group, we gay people must be judged by our leaders—by those who are gay and visible. For invisible, we remain in limbo—a myth, a person with no parents, no brothers, no sisters, no friends who are straight, no important positions in employment. A tenth of the nation supposedly composed of stereotypes and would-be seducers of children—and no offense meant to the stereotypes. But today, the black community is not judged by its friends, but by its black legislators and leaders. And we must give people the chance to judge us by our leaders and legislators. A gay person in office can set a tone, can command respect not only from the larger community, but also from the young people in our own community who need both examples and hope.

The first gay people we elect must be strong. They must not be content to sit in the back of the bus. They must not be content to accept pablum. They must be above wheeling and dealing. They must be—for the good of all of us—independent, unbought. The anger and the frustrations that some of us feel is because we are misunderstood, and friends can't feel the anger and frustration. They can sense it in us, but they can't feel it. Because a friend has never gone through what is known as coming out. I will never forget what it was like coming out and having nobody to look up toward. I remember the lack of hope—and our friends can't fulfill [that need].

I can't forget the looks on faces of people who've lost hope. Be they gay, be they seniors, be they blacks looking for an almost-impossible job, be they Latinos trying to explain their problems and aspirations in a tongue that's foreign to them.

I use the word *I* because I'm proud. I stand here tonight in front of my gay sisters, brothers, and friends because I'm proud of you. I think it's time that we have many legislators who are gay and proud of that fact and do not have to remain in the closet. I think that a gay person, up-front, will not walk away from a responsibility and be afraid of being tossed out of office. After Dade County, I walked among the angry and the frustrated night after night and I looked at their faces. In San Francisco, three days before Gay Pride Day, a person was killed just because he was gay. And that night, I walked among the sad and the frustrated at City Hall in San Francisco and later that night as they lit candles on Castro Street and stood in silence, reaching out for some symbolic thing that would give them hope. These were strong people, whose faces I knew from the shop, the streets, meetings and people who I never saw before but I knew. They were strong, but even they needed hope.

And the young gay people in the Altoona, Pennsylvanias, and the Richmond, Minnesotas, who are coming out and hear Anita Bryant on television—the only thing they have to look forward to is hope. You have to give them hope. Hope for a better world, hope for a better tomorrow, hope for a better place to come to if the pressures at home are too great. Hope that all will be all right. Without hope, not only gays, but the blacks, the seniors, the handicapped—the us'es, the us'es will give up.

If you help elect more gay people to the central committee and other offices, that gives a green light to all who feel disenfranchised, a green light to move forward. It means hope to a nation that has given up, because if a gay person makes it, the doors are open to everyone.

So if there is a message I have to give, it is that I've found one overriding thing about my personal election and it's the fact that if a gay person can be elected, it's a green light.

You and you and you, you have to give people hope.

Thank you very much.

VIRGINIA APUZZO (1941–)

When Bronx-native Ginny Apuzzo was ten, she proposed to her best friend Lucille, who didn't respond favorably. "That's when I learned of the 'love that dare not speak its name,'" she has said.[3] After college and graduate school, she entered the convent at the age of twenty-six but left after three years (in 1969) so she could do gay rights organizing the way she felt she must.

Apuzzo ran for office and dove into movement politics. In 1976, she lobbied to add a gay and lesbian plank to the Democratic Party platform (the plank was added in 1980) and fought for the National Organization for Women to list a similar plank as one of their four demands along with abortion, day care, and ERA, but NOW dropped gay rights when lobbying failed.

Apuzzo's experiences with the feminist movement of the second wave typify the exclusion many gay women felt—that their labor and support were desired, but not their issues or identities. "I felt like [as] a lesbian, I needed to have a guitar," Apuzzo once said. "You were fine if you had a guitar. If you played a little folk song, that was great. But if you were interested in lesbian feminist power, then you were going to embarrass [the straight feminists]."

3. *Virginia Apuzzo, interview by Kelly Anderson, Kingston, New York, June 2–3, 2004, Voices of Feminism Oral History Project, Sophia Smith Collection, Smith College.*

After becoming the director of the Gay and Lesbian Task Force during the AIDS crisis, Apuzzo made it clear that the epidemic "was and always has been a women's issue," as well as a health issue that intersects with homelessness, poverty, and racism. When she was appointed Assistant to the President for Administration and Management during the Clinton presidency, she became the highest ranking out lesbian government official in American history. Her work builds on the idea of hope, but adds in a crucial element of movement-building—power. The speech that follows, delivered at the end of the Reagan era, identifies the path to same-sex marriage. In reality, same-sex marriage itself wasn't her rallying point—and it isn't for many leaders within the movement—but she recognized that "the rights that accrue [via marriage] are significant and we're entitled to [them]."

Apuzzo's approach to lesbian and gay rights was intimately informed by feminism's claim on raising the status of women and destabilizing the false set of "norms" that dominated our understanding of men, women, and family. She knew that the more a homogeneous version of America was put forth, the harder it would be for anyone who defied that narrow path.

By the time she made this speech in 1988, at the National Gay and Lesbian Task Force "Creating Change" conference, AIDS had ravaged the gay community and framed how essential spousal benefits are. Gay, lesbian, and bisexual people began suing for domestic partner benefits. The *Village Voice* had started the practice of offering domestic partnership benefits in 1982, followed two years later by the city of Berkeley. Undermining that victory, the Supreme Court had ruled in 1986 in *Bower v. Hardwick* that homosexual sex is not protected under the right to privacy, and the misunderstanding of AIDS and who it affects was still a reliable scapegoat to justify antigay positions.

66   99

Creating Change
Virginia Apuzzo
November 20, 1988

It seems that it was never necessary to stake out the future quite as much as it is in this age of AIDS. In the past we believed that somehow we would have one.

It would be foolish to think that the experiences we have all shared around illness and death haven't had an impact on this community. But however profound our losses, our hope must exceed our grief. If we are to address the future with any seriousness, we cannot deny that our first order of business is to affirm our belief in our future.

Prior to the AIDS crisis, the white-male-dominated gay movement had an agenda that was largely libertarian . . . The agenda was often summed up as "getting government off our backs and . . . out of our bedrooms."

At the beginning of the AIDS crisis, we had behind us a decade of political activity which had focused on government as a wall of resistance. We studied that wall until we knew its every feature—but not what was on the other side.

I think we can agree that there has been a transformation that has taken place with regard to the agenda of the movement—namely, the way the community has come to see the role of government in the lives of its members.

With the onslaught of AIDS we continue to experience a significant political transformation. The concerns that we have been raising over the last several years are not code words for special interest items. We have spoken to matters related to the insurance industry, to the health care industry.

We have raised questions related to the role of schools in the face of the most threatening health crisis of our time, and we have insisted that the intransigence of our religious institutions not be permitted to cost the lives of their members.

We have raised for public repudiation the posture of a renegade Justice Department that would have conspired in the discrimination of those disabled by AIDS. Our position on the question of the HIV test, insurance, and employment, framed in the larger context of predicative tests, touches millions who are at risk for everything from Huntington's chorea and diabetes to hepatitis B.

Ours has been a call aimed at the very posture of government toward its citizens.

Our ability to make the essential linkages to other groups in our society on whom these issues also impinge will determine the extent to which we will complete the political transformation of the community—from an issue to a constituency. But there is more, much more.

If I could place a single question at the top of the agenda and ask the community to consider it before doing anything else, my question would be: do we really want to be a movement for social change in this society?

Unless and until that question is squarely faced, we

will bicker about tactics and strategy. We will be divided by differing objectives. We will be cut off from significant alliances.

Unless and until we address this question, we will be high on the rhetoric of our diversity . . . and low on coming to grips with how it does, in fact, separate us: black and white, male and female, rich and poor.

Unless and until we confront the implications of this question, we will see our movement as a series of events, and not a process; we will read these events as signposts with no agreement on where we are going or how to get there.

Unless and until we recognize the importance of this question, we run the risk of having the most fundamental meaning of our movement consigned to a nostalgic footnote in history.

Coming from the Bronx, I had to learn that politics and power isn't about tough-talking Damon Runyon characters with small IQs and big hearts—although I confess to having met a few. It tries instead to define what you can and cannot do while you are alive. Who you can and cannot be with some level of relaxed assurance. It is all of the social and economic limits, which must be pushed beyond artificial and self-serving boundaries. It is every limitation you will ever have to confront or may ultimately succumb to. For some it is possibly a limitation that could rob you of your capacity to rail against limitations. It is serious stuff.

It is therefore somewhat understandable that some would approach it making all kinds of assurances that what is being sought will not undermine the system, not rock the boat or upset the apple cart.

In my opinion, that's a mistake. A big mistake.

If we affirm our intention to be a movement for social change, we must get right to the heart of the matter and recognize that calling ourselves family, seeking to secure spousal benefits, giving birth to our own children, and seeking to provide foster care for the children of others is, quite simply, one of the most radical demands we make on the larger society.

I daresay that as significant as the litany of needs is, that this community has a legitimate right to demand. Items like: a federal lesbian and gay rights bill including housing, employment, and accommodations; immigration reform; a federal bias crime bill that includes sexual orientation; a sane AIDS program with the resources and compassion needed to finally address this epidemic.

And yet, each law or program cited can be won without ever challenging heterosexism at its core. And each must be won.

But after we have tallied up the score—victory upon victory—we will still be looking down the barrel of heterosexism. Unless we address this issue we will continue to pursue our legitimacy at the expense of our liberation.

If the division of the sexes and a heterosexual vision of what reality is are the principles by which this society defines itself, to ask it to embrace a feature of its humanity which runs counter to itself is to be a participant in a genuine revolution.

To prevail is to have brought major change. Consider the fact that one of the many things we share with the feminist movement is, not surprisingly, the same enemies for the same reasons. [These enemies] strive to establish the norm, and everything beyond that norm is fringe.

It is not a stupid strategy. The fewer the options available to members of the women's movement or the gay and lesbian movement, the greater the homogeneity in society—the greater the degree of sameness that exists, the greater the penalty for those who refuse to be homogenized. If the issue of our definition of relationships and family is as seminal as it appears, then it cannot be left to be fought solely in a political arena. Like any successful strategy for social change, it must be pursued on multiple fronts.

Major corporations have been approached with regard to personnel policies of nondiscrimination in employment. In the context of the AIDS crisis, they have been approached with regard to corporate giving.

But we have yet to see the potential of a coordinated campaign to make corporate America be part of the solution and not part of the problem where the lives of lesbians and gay men are concerned.

There are at least four major areas that could be outlined as having promise:

- Pursuing personnel policies with regard to nondiscrimination in employment. Much progress has been made here; more needs to be made.
- Corporate giving in two areas: one, with regard to political candidates they support; and two, with regard to gay and lesbian community projects that minimally parallel priorities in the corporations' existing patterns of giving.
- And, finally, spousal benefit programs on a nondiscriminatory basis.

A change of this magnitude would require education; I would begin with the professional personnel officers associations, giving workshops at conferences and conventions, working with legal organizations to develop model programs, and getting a maximum level of dialogue going in business journals and op-ed pages.

It would require an understanding of the opposition and not simply a dismissal of that opposition. It would require a willingness to analyze the opposition to determine how best to prevail in light of it.

It would require us entering the power-dominated world of corporate America with some grasp of what the coin of the realm is in that world.

If the division of the sexes and a heterosexual vision of what reality is are the principles by which this society defines itself, to ask it to embrace a feature of its humanity which runs counter to itself is to be a participant in a revolution. That's a choice we will have to consider confronting.

Finally, we have been fighting the good fight and there have been some significant victories. Perhaps the most significant is the ever-increasing number of us daring to live our lives visibly and with dignity as a twenty-four-hour-a-day, seven-day-a-week rebuke to the myths, the lies, and the distortions being peddled by the tin-horn moralists of the 1980s.

We are not about to retreat now. We will use every resource we have, call upon every commitment made to us, to respond to the threats that stalk our community: the ill and the dying, the tens of thousands whose lives have been stalled by fear, the victims of violence, the thousands who will die of alcohol- and substance-related deaths.

When we come together to speak with one voice, it must be with an agenda that does not permit this imperfect system to do what it does so very well. Namely, it cannot be permitted to simply shift the populations it selects to ignore.

In that spirit, let me close with a message I have repeated throughout the country—from the March on Washington to the smallest college gatherings. From the San Francisco Freedom Day rally to this year, when New Hampshire had its first lesbian and gay pride day celebration:

- Let us wed our promises to labor, each in our own way, for a community restored to health.
- Let us pledge never to allow convention to rob us of our just outrage at indifference to the dignity and value of human lives.
- Let us resolve that ours is a watch—a kind of tour of duty—that will not end with the passage of a lesbian and gay civil rights bill, though such a bill must be passed.

Ours is a watch that will not end with the treatment or cure for AIDS—though we will rejoice as never before. Ours is a watch that must be vigilant—vigilant for as long as ignorance can bully and for as long as justice is frail.

ANDREW SULLIVAN (1963–)

By the mid-1980s, a shocking new breed of gay luminary was emerging: the "normal" mainstream homosexual who desires inclusion more than revolution and freedom more than protection. Andrew Sullivan, a British contrarian, became editor of the political magazine the *New Republic* and quickly emerged as a leading conservative thinker. His 1989 *Atlantic* essay "Here Comes the Groom," reprinted below, made an early public case for gay marriage. His 1995 book *Virtually Normal: An Argument About Homosexuality*, continued this trajectory, arguing that marriage, which he calls "a profoundly humanizing, traditionalizing step," is "ultimately the only reform that truly matters."

Here Comes the Groom
Andrew Sullivan
August 28, 1989

Last month in New York, a court ruled that a gay lover had the right to stay in his deceased partner's rent-control apartment because the lover qualified as a member of the deceased's family. The ruling deftly annoyed almost everybody. Conservatives saw judicial activism in favor of gay rent control: three reasons to be appalled. Chastened liberals (such as the *New York Times* editorial page), while endorsing the recognition of gay relation-ships, also worried about the abuse of already stretched entitlements that the ruling threatened. What neither side quite contemplated is that they both might be right, and that the way to tackle the issue of unconventional relationships in conventional society is to try something both more radical and more conservative than put-ting courts in the business of deciding what is and is not a family. That alternative is the legalization of civil gay marriage. The New York rent-control case did not go anywhere near that far, which is the problem. The rent-control regulations merely stipulated that a "fam-ily" member had the right to remain in the apartment. The judge ruled that to all intents and purposes a gay lover is part of his lover's family, inasmuch as a "family" merely means an interwoven social life, emotional com-mitment, and some level of financial interdependence.

It's a principle now well established around the country. Several cities have "domestic partnership" laws, which allow relationships that do not fit into the category of heterosexual marriage to be registered with the city and qualify for benefits that up till now have been reserved for straight married couples. San Fran-cisco, Berkeley, Madison, and Los Angeles all have leg-islation, as does the politically correct Washington, DC, suburb, Takoma Park. In these cities, a variety of inter-personal arrangements qualify for health insurance, be-reavement leave, insurance, annuity and pension rights, housing rights (such as rent-control apartments), adop-tion and inheritance rights. Eventually, according to gay lobbying groups, the aim is to include federal income tax and veterans' benefits as well. A recent case even involved the right to use a family member's accumulated frequent-flier points. Gays are not the only beneficiaries; heterosexual "live-togethers" also qualify.

There's an argument, of course, that the current legal advantages extended to married people unfairly discriminate against people who've shaped their lives in less conventional arrangements. But it doesn't take a genius to see that enshrining in the law a vague principle like "domestic partnership" is an invitation to qualify at little personal cost for a vast array of entitlements otherwise kept crudely under control.

To be sure, potential DPs have to prove financial interdependence, shared living arrangements, and a commitment to mutual caring. But they don't need to have a sexual relationship or even closely mirror old-style marriage. In principle, an elderly woman and her live-in nurse could qualify. A couple of uneuphemistically confirmed bachelors could be DPs. So could two close college students, a pair of seminarians, or a couple of frat buddies. Left as it is, the concept of domestic partnership could open a Pandora's box of litigation and subjective judicial decision-making about who qualifies. You either are or are not married; it's not a complex question. Whether you are in a "domestic partnership" is not so clear.

More important, the concept of domestic partnership chips away at the prestige of traditional relationships and undermines the priority we give to them. The priority is not necessarily a product of heterosexism. Consider heterosexual couples. Society has good reason to extend legal advantages to heterosexuals who choose the formal sanction of marriage over simply living together. They make a deeper commitment to one another and to society; in exchange, society extends certain benefits to them. Marriage provides an anchor, if an arbitrary and weak one, in the chaos of sex and relationships to which we are all prone. It provides a mechanism for emotional stability, economic security, and the healthy rearing of the next generation. We rig the law in its favor not because we disparage all forms of relationship other than the nuclear family, but because we recognize that not to promote marriage would be to ask too much of human virtue. In the context of the weakened family's effect upon the poor, it might also invite social disintegration. One of the worst products of the New Right's "family values" campaign is that its extremism and hatred of diversity has disguised this more measured and more convincing case for the importance of the marital bond.

The concept of domestic partnership ignores these concerns, indeed directly attacks them. This is a pity, since one of its most important objectives—providing some civil recognition for gay relationships—is a noble cause and one completely compatible with the defense of the family. But the way to go about it is not to undermine straight marriage; it is to legalize old-style marriage for gays.

The gay movement has ducked the issue primarily out of fear of division. Much of the gay leadership clings to notions of gay life as essentially outsider, antibourgeois, radical. Marriage, for them, is co-optation into straight society. For the Stonewall generation, it is hard to see how this vision of conflict will ever fundamentally change. But for many other gays—my guess, a majority—

while they don't deny the importance of rebellion twenty years ago and are grateful for what was done, there's now the sense of a new opportunity. A need to rebel has quietly ceded to a desire to belong. To be gay and to be bourgeois no longer seems such an absurd proposition. Certainly since AIDS, to be gay and to be responsible has become a necessity.

Gay marriage squares several circles at the heart of the domestic partnership debate. Unlike domestic partnership, it allows for recognition of gay relationships, while casting no aspersions on traditional marriage. It merely asks that gays be allowed to join in. Unlike domestic partnership, it doesn't open up avenues for heterosexuals to get benefits without the responsibilities of marriage, or a nightmare of definitional litigation. And unlike domestic partnership, it harnesses to an already established social convention the yearnings for stability and acceptance among a fast-maturing gay community.

Gay marriage also places more responsibilities upon gays; it says for the first time that gay relationships are not better or worse than straight relationships, and that the same is expected of them. And it's clear and dignified. There's a legal benefit to a clear, common symbol of commitment. There's also a personal benefit. One of the ironies of domestic partnership is that it's not only more complicated than marriage, it's more demanding, requiring an elaborate statement of intent to qualify. It amounts to a substantial invasion of privacy. Why, after all, should gays be required to prove commitment before they get married in a way we would never dream of asking of straights?

Legalizing gay marriage would offer homosexuals the

same deal society now offers heterosexuals: general social approval and specific legal advantages in exchange for a deeper and harder-to-extract-yourself-from commitment to another human being. Like straight marriage, it would foster social cohesion, emotional security, and economic prudence. Since there's no reason gays should not be allowed to adopt or be foster parents, it could also help nurture children. And its introduction would not be some sort of radical break with social custom. As it has become more acceptable for gay people to acknowledge their loves publicly, more and more have committed themselves to one another for life in full view of their families and their friends. A law institutionalizing gay marriage would merely reinforce a healthy social trend. It would also, in the wake of AIDS, qualify as a genuine public health measure. Those conservatives who deplore promiscuity among some homosexuals should be among the first to support it. Burke could have written a powerful case for it.

The argument that gay marriage would subtly undermine the unique legitimacy of straight marriage is based upon a fallacy. For heterosexuals, straight marriage would remain the most significant—and only—legal social bond. Gay marriage could only delegitimize straight marriage if it were a real alternative to it, and this is clearly not true. To put it bluntly, there's precious little evidence that straights could be persuaded by any law to have sex with—let alone marry—someone of their own sex. The only possible effect of this sort would be to persuade gay men and women who force themselves into heterosexual marriage (often at appalling cost to themselves and their families) to find a focus for their family instincts in a more personally positive environment. But this is clearly a plus, not a minus: gay marriage could both avoid a lot of tortured families and create the possibility for many happier ones. It is not, in short, a denial of family values. It's an extension of them.

Of course, some would claim that any legal recognition of homosexuality is a de facto attack upon heterosexuality. But even the most hardened conservatives recognize that gays are a permanent minority and aren't likely to go away. Since persecution is not an option in civilized society, why not coax gays into traditional values rather than rain incoherently against them?

There's a less elaborate argument for gay marriage: it's good for gays. It provides role models for young gay people who, after the exhilaration of coming out, can easily lapse into short-term relationships and insecurity with no tangible goal in sight. My own guess is that most gays would embrace such a goal with as much (if not more) commitment as straights. Even in our society as it is, many lesbian relationships are virtual textbook cases of monogamous commitment. Legal gay marriage could also help bridge the gulf often found between gays and their parents. It could bring the essence of gay life— a gay couple—into the heart of the traditional straight family in a way the family can most understand and the gay offspring can most easily acknowledge. It could do as much to heal the gay-straight rift as any amount of gay rights legislation.

If these arguments sound socially conservative, that's no accident. It's one of the richest ironies of our society's blind spot toward gays that essentially conservative social goals should have the appearance of being so radical. But gay marriage is not a radical step. It avoids the mess of domestic partnership; it is humane; it is conservative in the best sense of the word. It's also about relationships. Given that gay relationships will always exist, what possible social goal is advanced by framing the law so as to encourage those relationships to be unfaithful, undeveloped, and insecure?

PART II

THE PERSONAL BECOMES POLITICAL

DAVID MIXNER (1946–)

" I have a vision and you are part of it," then candidate Bill Clinton promised a largely gay audience in Los Angeles on May 18, 1992. It was the first time a serious contender vowed to include gay rights and gay people in the American conversation. By this time, David Mixner, the founder of Municipal Elections Committee of Los Angeles (MECLA) PAC, had been raising money for candidates for years, but he was accustomed to having checks returned to him if they could be traced to openly gay sources. Here, it appeared, was a politician who could embrace the gay community. Indeed, Clinton campaigned on the promise to allow all citizens to serve in the US military regardless of sexual orientation, overturning a long-term ban on gays in the military and vowing to direct more money to research and services for people with AIDS.

Joy quickly turned to shock and sadness as President Clinton, facing pressure from members of the military, Congress, and the public signed on to "Don't Ask, Don't Tell"—a compromise that enabled gay people to serve, as long as they were closeted. In Mixner's 1993 speech that follows, he exhorts President Clinton to make history, not sign away people's freedom for the sake of political expediency. Specifically, President Clinton proposed having barracks segregated by sexuality. Sadly, a mere eight months after this speech in 1993, the president signed "Don't Ask, Don't Tell" into law, where it remained until September 20, 2011. Mixner's March 1993 speech at the Metropolitan Community Church in Dallas, Texas, begins with visibility, but moves quickly to the demand for full participation in all of the institutions the US holds sacred. While the issue of that election cycle was the military, it set the stage for extending the rights and responsibilities of marriage to gay people.

66 *The Story of Self-Hatred* 99
David Mixner
March 27, 1993

Brothers and sisters: It is rare that I have the (opportunity) to speak so urgently among people for whom I have so much love. It is difficult to speak truth and know that it might bring pain between old friends. But today I must . . .

Because for us, truth is our sword. For us, our unity in numbers is our army. For us, our AIDS dead have inspired in us courage and determination that we ourselves did not know existed.

We now get to prepare for the battle that we have long sought: A national debate that will eventually lead to our freedom. A national debate that no longer treats us as a fringe sideshow in American politics but as an emerging and powerful civil rights movement. The future of the next generations of lesbians and gays will be decided by us—not by weak leaders, not by ballot box terrorism, not by religious fanatics who use our freedom as a tool to build their bank accounts, but rather by our strength and our courage.

History will not present us with a more historical movement than now. Each one of us will be judged by future generations by our actions in the next several months and years. If, as a family, we rise to the challenge, we truly have the opportunity to change years of oppression into a future filled with hope.

Where do we begin? Where do we find such courage? How do we build the commitment and determination that will last us through these difficult and challenging years?

We begin with our gayness. We find courage in who we are. We build our commitment by a determination that not one more generation of gays and lesbians will ever have to suffer the pangs of discrimination and self-hatred. We will no longer deny our young their dreams.

I am often asked why it is so important for me to publicly and repeatedly declare my sexuality. As I stand here among the leaders of our church, I want you to know who I am. I am a spiritual person. Each morning I pray before I begin my day. In my prayers I thank God for making me a gay person. I thank God for allowing me one more day to join my brothers and sisters in battle. I ask God for the strength to join with you in fighting for our freedom, and I ask my God to give me the time to see our young celebrate in that freedom.

You see, I used to be ashamed. I wanted to kill myself. I deferred my dreams and adapted to a life offering less of myself to this world instead of more. I felt alone and alienated and I felt terribly afraid. Then, because of the actions of a few brave drag queens, I saw strength and hope. I started to dream again. I felt pride. I felt your love and support. I could say I am gay and proud—not without fear, but I could say it.

Then came AIDS. Death and devastation. Our lives became hospital rooms, home-care delivery systems, life-support machines, and funerals. I buried 189 of my friends. I fought so that in their illness they would not be persecuted by our own government. I once again felt despair and lost hope. We grew weary and wondered if those years of fleeting liberation in the 1970s were all that we would know of freedom. We joined together in the streets, in the voting booths, in our service centers, and in our churches to support each other and to fight back.

Then came President Clinton.

Allow me to be frank and honest about our president. Our journey together as a community with the president has been an intoxicating one. We have found once again our united voice. We have discovered our own power. We raised money, walked precincts, and begged our families, employers, and friends to join us in ending our twelve years of darkness. We started to believe in ourselves again. We dreamed again of a future.

He was elected. He proceeded to keep his promises, not to us as a special interest group, but to us as Americans who wanted to participate fully in our society, who at last would be allowed to contribute our skills and talents as an open and free people.

In this process of keeping his promise to us, he encountered what we experience every day of our lives—outright bigotry and homophobia! The voices of the past rose to deny us of our moment of freedom. Military leaders are fighting to keep ancient apartheid laws on the books and to resist ending fifty years of repression and persecution. They frighten our neighbors with the big lie. They paint pictures that contain only dark colors. They resort to the same bigoted arguments that have been used for centuries to deny every emerging minority their freedom and equal rights. They sought the cover of legitimacy in Armed Forces chairperson Sam Nunn. Let me be clear about Senator Nunn. Let us educate those people, including some in the administration, that this is not an enlightened man. Listen to me carefully. Sam Nunn is our George Wallace. He is an old-fashioned bigot who will abuse his power to deny us our freedom. His hatred runs so deep that he is willing to jeopardize the nation's economic hopes in order to deny freedom to millions. His anger is so fierce that he will focus his energy on stopping us from serving our country while the world around him in Russia and Bosnia falls to pieces. This man does not deserve the respectability that he has been accorded by so many. He has chosen hate over love . . . fear over enlightenment . . . and division over unity. We will not quake in his presence. We will not fear him. We will not give him the power to determine our future.

This brings us back to our president. We were proud to stand by his side during this last campaign. We wept when he mentioned the words *gay* and *lesbian* at the convention and *AIDS* on election night. We pinched ourselves in disbelief when he came and gave a gay rights speech in Los Angeles. We were filled with hope and dreams when the poet at the inauguration dared to speak our name. But for the president too—his moment has arrived.

Mr. President, our friend, hear us carefully. Only our

total freedom will do. There can be no further compromises with our dreams, our rights, and our futures. An executive order issued without moral authority and decisive leadership is only a piece of paper. An executive order issued with moral authority and decisive leadership is history. Now is the time that will decide if you will sit with the great emancipator Abraham Lincoln as a man who freed millions or if you will go down in history as a man who, for political expediency, negotiated our freedom away in the backrooms of Congress. It is your choice. We have made ours. We will fight however long it takes to be free. Will you join us in creating a debate steeped in morality and not fear; one that appeals to the best that this nation has to offer, not the worst; and one where your leadership will enlighten, not distort? It is your call. Now is the time . . . not June 15, not July 15, not next year when it will be too late . . . but *now!*

Mr. President, do not give dignity to false compromises. Do not embrace the Vatican approach to homosexuality. What kind of freedom is it when you ask us to either remain silent or, if we do speak of our sexuality, give up the right to practice it in the privacy of our own homes? This is unacceptable.

Mr. President, do not negotiate our freedom away. Separate assignments and separate units is no more than old-fashioned segregation. No rhetoric can hide the fact that separating a whole group of American citizens because of who they are is nothing more than segregation. Bigotry that wears a uniform is nothing more than a uniform with a hood. Segregation is morally repugnant to us and we will never, ever accept segregation as a sign of progress.

Mr. President, you can make our road to freedom easier. You can speak to this nation of unity, of our unused talents and skills, and of our suffering. You can educate senators. You can provide the moral high ground that Senator Nunn is stealing from us. You can provide decisive leadership, courage, and most of all our freedom. But make no mistake—with or without you, we will be free. We will win and we will prevail.

Mr. President, do not underestimate our determination and our courage. We are willing to lose our jobs for freedom. We are willing, if necessary, to go to jail. We are willing to give our last cent for freedom. We are willing to do anything except return to the slavery of self-hatred and low self-esteem.

My friends, in closing, don't forget what it used to be like. So many of our friends who could share with us the horrible oppression of self-hatred have passed on—but each of us here knows it. We know of the past lies to our families and friends . . . we know of the fear at work . . . we know of deferring our dreams . . . we know of being ashamed of those we loved the most . . . we know of the attempted suicides, and we know what each and every one of us had to overcome to even be here in this room. We can't go back to that. We can't retreat at the first sound of battle. We must join together to fight and—make no mistake about it—to win.

Thank you very much.

DEFENSE OF MARRIAGE ACT
CONGRESSIONAL DEBATES

I n 1996, Congress moved to vote on a bill called the Defense of Marriage Act. The law stated, in part:

Section 2. Powers reserved to the states
No State, territory, or possession of the United States, or Indian tribe, shall be required to give effect to any public act, record, or judicial proceeding of any other State, territory, possession, or tribe respecting a relationship between persons of the same sex that is treated as a marriage under the laws of such other State, territory, possession, or tribe, or a right or claim arising from such relationship.

Section 3. Definition of marriage
In determining the meaning of any Act of Congress, or of any ruling, regulation, or interpretation of the various administrative bureaus and agencies of the United States, the word "marriage" means only a legal union between one man and one woman as husband and wife, and the word "spouse" refers only to a person of the opposite sex who is a husband or a wife.

It sailed though the vote, 342 to 67 in the House and 85 to 14 in the Senate, and was signed into law on September 21, 1996. These are excerpts of testimony from politicians who voted *against* DOMA.

" *Congressional Debate on DOMA* "
Patrick Kennedy (D-RI), Nancy Pelosi (D-CA),
Luis Gutierrez (D-IL), Lynn Woolsey (D-CA),
Lynn Rivers (D-MI), Jerrold Nadler (D-NY),
Samuel Farr (D-CA), John Lewis (D-GA),
Sheila Jackson Lee (D-TX), Jim McDermott (D-WA),
Neil Abercrombie (D-HI)
July 11, 1996

Mr. Patrick Kennedy, Democrat, of Rhode Island:
Mr. Chairman, this debate really is about a simple question, a question of equal rights. Marriage is a basic right. It is a basic human right. Love and commitment are essential pillars of marriage. They are qualities that do not discriminate on account of gender. It is not right for this Congress to step in and to intrude into the private relationships and the most personal decisions of our constituencies. Love and commitment can exist between a man and a woman and it can and does exist between men and between women.

Proponents of this curiously titled bill say that we need legislation to protect the family. Nothing could be further from the truth. Families are not threatened when two adults who love each other make a lifelong commitment to one another. Families will not fall apart if gay men and women are allowed to marry, if they are allowed the same basic legal right to marry that is already enjoyed by heterosexuals.

This is not about defending marriage. It is about finding an enemy. It is not about marital union. It is about disunion, about dividing one group of Americans against another. This bill is unconstitutional, this bill is unfair, and the spirit behind this bill further fans the flames of prejudice and bigotry that this 104th Congress has done a pretty good job at fanning thus far.

I think it is a travesty that people would bring this bill out simply to polarize Americans even further. Instead of bringing love and commitment and worshiping that in our society, this bill sows the seeds of division and hatred amongst people. I think that is a very unfortunate thing.

Ms. Nancy Pelosi, Democrat, of California:
Mr. Chairman, I thank the gentleman for yielding me this time and for his strong leadership on this important issue and other issues of civil and human rights in this country and throughout the world.

Mr. Chairman, I rise in strong opposition to this ill-named Defense of Marriage Act and I do so on the basis of conscience, Constitution, and constituency.

This legislation in terms of the Constitution, I believe, violates the spirit of the Constitution's "full faith and credit" clause as well as its equal protection provisions. It also is quite ironic to me that the Republican Party, which is a strong advocate for states' rights, now wants to override the will of the states, and this is all in the hypothetical at that.

As a matter of conscience, I am opposed to this legislation because I believe it is a blatant act of discrimination. It is also disappointing that it is happening at this time because last week on the Fourth of July we celebrated our country's independence and our country's greatness. This week we are acting to diminish that greatness by saying to some members of our society that they are not equal under the law. Who is next? This bill is an insult to gays and lesbians in our country. Who is next? That brings me to my constituency.

I have the privilege of representing the most diverse population of any district in the country. I know there will be those who say their districts are as diverse, but I do not think anyone's is more diverse than mine. In my district, I can easily see and say that the beauty is in the mix. I want to be sure that the power is also in the mix, the power for all of those different people to make their own decisions about their personal lives, the power for them to reach their own fulfillment, newcomer or old guard, black, brown, white, or yellow, gay or lesbian.

Those decisions and that fulfillment include those affecting their life, liberty, and pursuit of happiness. We value family in our community as a source of strength to our country and a source of comfort to our people. What constitutes that family is an individual and personal decision. But it is for all a place where people find love and support. If that happens to be with people living together of the same sex or of different sex, if it happens platonically or not, if it happens that they find comfort and love and support, God bless them.

Let me tell you about two very special constituents of mine who have lived together for over twenty-five years. Their commitment, their love, and their happiness are a source of strength to all who know them. Their relationship—I hold this up so you can all see—is not a threat to anyone's marriage. This is Phyllis Lyons and Del Martin.[4] Phyllis has two grandchildren. Phyllis and Del have been leaders in our community and command the respect of all who know them. Why should they not be able to share each other's health and bereavement benefits? Why should they not be able to visit each other in the hospital in case of accident or in case of illness? I know people will say, you can sign up in advance and tell the doctor before you go in for the operation. That does not happen if you are in an accident. Why should they not be able to share a financial relationship inheritance, immigration—the list goes on and on.

Why should they not have the full protection of the law? All of our community in our area are in debt to Phyllis and Del for their contribution to the community, serving on commissions . . . they have been officially recognized over and over again in the course of their years of service. Tonight I am again in their debt for allowing me to share their personal history with you. I thank them for doing that, and I say to all of you, if you knew Phyllis and Del and many hundreds of thousands of people that I know like them, why would you not want them to be treated equally?

But I ask you to make a more personal question of yourselves. Should you find yourself in a situation where your children or your close relatives or your close friends find solace, happiness, comfort, love, support in a relationship that is appropriate for them, would you not want them to have the legal recognition that they deserve? It is not, again, a threat to anyone.

Mr. Chairman, I wish I could go into what is a threat

---

4. *Phyllis Lyons and Del Martin were the first people to marry in San Francisco when Mayor Gavin Newsom began issuing licenses.*

to marriage in this country, but with that I urge my colleagues to think carefully before discriminating against anyone in this country. I urge our colleagues to vote no on this legislation.

Mr. Luis Gutierrez, Democrat, of Illinois:

Mr. Chairman, without question, we've heard some puzzling arguments in favor of the Defense of Marriage Act.

But at least one good thing has come from this debate: I think everyone understands better when to take my Republican friends seriously and when they are just having a good laugh at the expense of the American people.

I now realize that my friends on the other side of the aisle aren't the least bit serious when they talk about how important it is for the federal government not to interfere in the lives of our people.

I understand that they are just kidding—just teasing us—when they stress the importance of taking power out of Washington and giving it to local officials.

And now I know that their biggest joke of all is that old line about the importance of family values—all that talk about encouraging people to care about and be committed to each other.

Because the bill that most of my friends on the other side of the aisle are supporting tonight represents the polar opposite of all those lofty goals we've heard them talk so much about.

The misleadingly titled Defense of Marriage Act is the ultimate in Washington bureaucracy dictating to the American people how they should live their lives.

And it is an outstanding example of telling state officials how they should legislate and make policy.

This should be a simple issue. Unfortunately, for many of my colleagues on the other side of the aisle, that simple issue is politics. It's as simple as exploiting fears and promoting prejudice.

But something more important than looking for a few extra votes should be simple too: seeking fairness. Seeking an America where all people are treated the same under the law, in every aspect of their lives—from choosing where they live to who they marry.

And one more thing should be simple: promoting freedom. Making sure that all Americans have the freedom to live their personal lives in exactly the way they choose. Without being discriminated against. Without being stopped or harassed by a meddling federal government. Without being prevented by legislators from deciding what is best for them.

I think the debate we hear tonight is the very reason so many Americans are troubled by politicians exploiting the idea of "family values." I don't know many Americans—regardless of their political party, race, religion, or sexual orientation—who don't believe that family values are vitally important. But I also don't know many Americans who want a couple of hundred politicians in Washington to impose their values on everyone else's families.

Let me tell you about some very basic values I think we're talking about when we stand up against this bill: The values of people who love each other. People who share each other's lives. People who care about their future and the future of those around them. People who want to make a commitment that is legal and official and is important to them.

To me, that sounds like family values. And all of the noise we hear on the other side of the aisle sounds like politics as usual.

I encourage my colleagues in the House today, and I don't say this very often—give my Republican friends what they say they want. Real family values. And more local control. And a federal government that stays out of Americans' lives.

There's only one way to do that: vote to defeat the Defense of Marriage Act.

Ms. Lynn Woolsey, Democrat, of California:
Mr. Chairman, H.R. 3396 outlaws something that does not even exist. It tramples over the Constitution. It flies in the face of states' rights, and it plays into the hands of the radical right, those who are trying to divide our country by scapegoating gays and lesbians. But let us move beyond the bill's numerous flaws and look at how it will affect American families. Let us look at what it will mean to *my* family.

Last month my youngest son married a wonderful young woman. As friends and family gathered to celebrate their commitment to each other, the State of California also granted them the legal benefits of marriage. This bill, however, would ensure that another of my sons will never have the same options nor the protections that come with marriage. In fact, even the most basic rights of marriage that my youngest son already takes for granted, such as the ability to visit his spouse in a hospital, could be denied to his brother, denied because of his sexual orientation.

Mr. Chairman, let us not reduce ourselves to being

pawns for the radical right. Let us not turn the House of Representatives into a political convention for extremists. For once let us reject fear, embrace tolerance, and move this nation forward without leaving anyone behind. I urge my colleagues to defeat this really mean-spirited bill.

Ms. Lynn Rivers, Democrat, of Michigan:
Mr. Chairman, I rise in opposition to this bill and I oppose it with both my head and my heart. My head, because my brain and my legal training tell me that there are constitutional flaws in this particular bill. My heart speaks even more strongly to tell me that this is wrong. Wrong because in America, rights are not for some but not for others. We do not have one-half citizenship or three-quarters citizenship for some people and different kinds of citizenship for another. We treat all of our citizens the same.

I took a look at the marriage vows, because I tried to decide what it is exactly that we want to keep people from having under this bill. When you take generic wedding vows that are accepted in many churches you find words like this: I, *So-and-So, take you to be my wedded husband, wife, to have and to hold.* And I thought, *to have and to hold,* which people is it that we want to forbid to have a committed relationship, to be sustained by the love of another person?

For better or worse, I ask again, which people are there that we want to make sure should not have a soul mate, a partner in life's struggle, someone to laugh with, someone to cry with, someone to work with, to improve their lives, to support one another through good times and bad?

I looked at the words "in sickness and in health" and I asked myself, what people does the government want to keep from having a partner who will nurture them, who will nurse them, who will wipe their brow, who will hold their hand when they are ill? I could not find any.

I looked at the words "to love and to cherish" and I asked myself, who does the government want to keep from being the center of another person's life? Who do we want to stop from being hugged, held, adored?

I looked at the words "I promise to be faithful to you until death parts us" and I asked myself, as a matter of public policy, who do we want to forbid from a monogamous promise? And given the comments made earlier about promiscuity, I cannot imagine who that would be.

Love is not a zero-sum game, Mr. Chairman. One couple's love is not a threat to another. Today's marriages are threatened by a lack of commitment, a lack of maturity, and a lack of fidelity. To argue anything else is specious.

Mr. Jerrold Nadler, Democrat, of New York:
Mr. Chairman, we began our national life by declaring that all men are created equal. We did not really mean it. We meant that all white men of property are created equal. The history of this country is largely the history of expanding that definition to all white men, to white men and black men, to white men and black men and white women and black women. We have achieved all that, but we said we want to achieve all that. We are just beginning to go down that road for gay and lesbian people. We still permit discrimination by law. We are

just beginning to expand that definition, and we will.

The arguments against gay and lesbian marriage are essentially the same arguments that we used to hear against black-white marriages. We had antimiscegenation laws in this country. I have no doubt that one day we will permit in every state in this union, and we will celebrate, gay and lesbian marriages. One day we will look back and wonder why it was ever thought controversial to allow two people who wanted to share each other's lives in a committed, monogamous relationship to undertake the obligations and benefits of marriage, why it was ever thought that allowing gay and lesbian people to visit each other in the hospital or to share each other's pension rights posed a threat to marriages of heterosexual people.

But the bill before us today is not designed to solve a real problem. It is designed to appeal to fear and prejudice and hatred and bigotry. It is also a fraud.

We are told we must pass this bill to protect our states from being compelled by the Constitution's "full faith and credit" clause to recognize same-sex marriages entered into in Hawaii. Aside from the fact they were a year or two away from Hawaii making any such decision, the "full faith and credit" clause does not compel or would not compel states to do such a thing. The public policy exception that today allows New York or Connecticut to refuse to recognize a fifteen-year-old marriage entered into in states which permit fifteen-year-old marriages would permit states on public policy grounds not to recognize same-sex marriages if they choose not to. So that section of the bill is unnecessary.

But the other section of the bill, the section that defines marriage in federal law for the first time and says to any state, "No matter what you do, whether you do it by referendum or by public decision or by legislative action, the federal government won't recognize a marriage contracted in your state if we don't like the definition; we are going to trample the states' rights," shows exactly where this bill is coming from. We are going to say those are second-class marriages because we overruled New York or Connecticut or Hawaii or whoever decides to do that.

Why do we want to start down the road of a federal marriage law? This bill, Mr. Chairman, defends against a nonexistent threat. Marriages in this country are threatened by a 50 percent divorce rate, by drugs, by alcoholism, by gambling, by immaturity, by lots of things, but not by allowing gay or lesbian couples to formalize their relationships and pursue their happiness.

Mr. Chairman, this is a despicable bill, and I urge its defeat.

Mr. Samuel Farr, Democrat, of California:
Mr. Chairman, I thank the gentleman from Massachusetts for yielding. As one of the great leaders of human rights issues, I appreciate his time.

I cannot believe that we call ourselves lawmakers. I think we fail to ask ourselves what is broke here that needs fixing. Our country has just gone through 220 years without federal law on marriages. Think about it. We do not have a federal marriage license. People get married under state law. Some states allow people to marry cousins. Some states allow persons committing statutory rape to have the rape dropped if they marry the person. States do not regulate how many times someone can get married, they do not regulate how many times someone can get a divorce.

So why is this bill called the Defense of Marriage Act? It does not improve marriages, and it takes away states' rights.

This bill is not about marriage, because the federal government does not marry people. This bill is about meanness, it is about taking away states' right to enact a law that would allow an elderly man or an elderly woman, maybe a grandmother, even someone's grandfather, from receiving the benefits or giving benefits to a caretaker of the same sex who they may marry for only the reasons of being able to inherit property. It says that the only way someone can leave Social Security benefits or medical care benefits or federal estate tax deductions is if they married someone of the opposite sex. Elderly people often live together with friends of the same sex. If a state wants to honor that arrangement for tax benefit purposes equal to marriage, this bill would ban it.

My wife and I have raised our daughter in a loving supportive relationship. Our daughter recently asked us, "Why is your generation so homophobic?" I told her that it was the last civil rights battle in America. She said, "I hope you solve it because for our generation, it's no big deal."

Let us listen to our elderly, let us listen to our youth; make laws that help people, not hurt them. Reject this mean-spirited bill.

Mr. John Lewis, Democrat, of Georgia:
Mr. Chairman, I want to thank my friend and colleague for yielding me the time.

Let me say to the gentleman that when I was growing up in the South during the 1940s and the 1950s, the
great majority of the people in that region believed that
black people should not be able to enter places of public
accommodation, and they felt that black people should
not be able to register to vote, and many people felt that
was right—but that was wrong. I think as politicians, as
elected officials, we should not only follow but we must
lead, lead our districts, not put our fingers into the wind
to see which way the air is blowing, but be leaders.

Mr. Chairman, this is a mean bill. It is cruel. This
bill seeks to divide our nation, turn Americans against
Americans, sow the seeds of fear, hatred, and intolerance. Let us remember the Preamble of the Declaration
of Independence: *We hold these truths to be self-evident, that all
men are created equal, that they are endowed by their Creator with
certain unalienable Rights, that among these are Life, Liberty and
the pursuit of Happiness.*

This bill is a slap in the face of the Declaration of Independence. It denies gay men and women the right to
liberty and the pursuit of happiness. Marriage is a basic
human right. You cannot tell people they cannot fall in
love. Dr. Martin Luther King Jr. used to say when people
talked about interracial marriage, and I quote, "Races
do not fall in love and get married. Individuals fall in
love and get married."

Why do you not want your fellow men and women,
your fellow Americans, to be happy? Why do you attack
them? Why do you want to destroy the love they hold
in their hearts? Why do you want to crush their hopes,
their dreams, their longings, their aspirations?

We are talking about human beings, people like you,

people who want to get married, buy a house, and spend their lives with the one they love. They have done no wrong. I will not turn my back on another American. I will not oppress my fellow human beings. I have fought too hard and too long against discrimination based on race and color not to stand up against discrimination based on sexual orientation.

Mr. Chairman, I have known racism. I have known bigotry. This bill stinks of the same fear, hatred, and intolerance. It should not be called the Defense of Marriage Act. It should be called the Defense of Mean-Spirited Bigots Act.

I urge my colleagues to oppose this bill, to have the courage to do what is right. This bill appeals to our worst fears and emotions. It encourages hatred of our fellow Americans for political advantage. Every word, every purpose, every message is wrong. It is not the right thing to do, to divide Americans.

We are moving toward the twenty-first century. Let us come together and create one nation, one people, one family, one house, the American house, the American family, the American nation.

Ms. Sheila Jackson Lee, Democrat, of Texas:
Mr. Chairman, I am opposed to the rule for the so-called Defense of Marriage Act. The rule allows only two amendments to this very unnecessary piece of legislation. In committee, an attempt by Congresswoman Schroeder and myself to include the words *nonadulterous* and *monogamous* to the definition of marriage in the bill was rejected, and because this is a modified closed rule we cannot offer this change today.

No one can deny that the family as an institution has changed dramatically since the days when our own parents were children. Today, there is no single definition of family that applies to all individuals. A family may be made up of two parents and their children, grandparents caring for grandchildren, single mothers or single fathers raising their children, couples without children, foster parents and foster children, or individuals of the same sex living together and sharing their lives as a couple. How their relationships are handled should be left to the states. This legislation takes the right of the states away.

We need to respect the human rights of all these American families. We should not make laws which are based on an antiquated notion of what constitutes a family. This unnecessary legislation patently disregards the Fourteenth Amendment provision that provides equal protection under the law to all Americans. I believe this legislation has been rushed forward with little thought and reason.

As a wife and a mother, I believe in the human family. The institution of marriage should be cherished and respected. However, same-sex relationships allow human beings to express their attitude of caring for each other. Recognized same-sex relationships simply allow individuals living together and loving each other to be entitled to the rights associated with a loving and caring relationship.

This legislation would define marriage as "a legal union between one man and one woman as husband and wife." The word *spouse* would refer "only to a person of the opposite sex who is a husband or a wife."

Never before has the federal government attempted to define either *marriage* or *spouse*. This has, and continues to be, the role of the states and they have done it well for the past two hundred years. It is beyond the responsibility of the federal government to define marriage and impose that definition on the states.

Furthermore, even if (as the bill's sponsors claim) the federal government needs to step in to clarify differing definitions between states, this legislation is premature. Same-sex marriage is not legal in any state. Hawaii is unlikely to decide the issue of same-sex marriage for at least two years, so this legislation attacks an issue which is not yet ripe. The only reasons to deal with it now is to make it a political controversy.

Finally, since we are being forced to consider this legislation, I do not see why we could not attach the Employment Non-Discrimination Act (ENDA) to this legislation. This long-awaited legislation would extend federal employment discrimination protections to include sexual orientation, providing basic protection to ensure fairness in the workplace for Americans who are currently denied equal protection under the law. If we are going to consider this type of legislation, a consideration of ENDA should be included. This rule does not allow for such a consideration. I urge my colleagues to vote down this rule. Thank you.

Mr. Jim McDermott, Democrat, of Washington:
Mr. Chairman, I rise to marvel at the wisdom of Congress. We have done such a wonderful job over these past two years that we are ready to take on the awesome task of matchmaking for all citizens of the United States.

The legislation we are debating now dictates to them who they can love and spend their lives with in order to benefit from the rights guaranteed by the Constitution and the legal benefits of our laws—civil laws governing marriage and divorce that have previously been the province of the states.

Have we nothing better to do with our time?

Marriage is a personal matter. Marriage is about two people coming together to love and support each other. Why should Congress interfere in this very personal decision?

It was less than thirty years ago that our courts ruled it unconstitutional for the states to ban marriage between persons of different ethnic backgrounds. Have we learned so little in the last thirty years?

This bill has nothing to do with family values or protecting the institution of marriage. It is a political game to obscure the real issues behind the failure of marriages and to divide Americans in an election year.

It is an attempt to fan the coals of bigotry and hatred to try to gain a few votes. The institution of marriage will not be saved to strengthened by increasing hate between our citizens.

This is not a religious issue. Each of the numerous religions practiced in America is free to perform the rites of marriage in accordance with its tenets. Many marriages between persons of the same gender have been blessed by their religions—in all fifty states. This is purely and simply a civil matter—whether the federal government should decide for its citizens which of these unions to recognize and with whom citizens may share their vows of marriage.

Nor is this a moral issue. The only moral question before us is whether it is moral to use this legislation to foster prejudice and misinformation among our citizens for political gain.

I suggest we turn our attention to creating conditions that foster relationships between people in which they care for each other. To quote Ecclesiastes 4:9–10, *Two are better than one. If one falls down, his friend can help him up.*

The Reverend Billy Graham used that biblical quote to justify marriage. Reverend Graham stated, "Nowhere is this truer than in marriage when sickness or other problems come. One of the reasons God has given marriage to us is for times like this."

It is with marriage that our society makes it a little easier to survive and obtain fulfillment.

Let's turn our efforts to making life a little easier for people by giving them all equal opportunities to love and help each other.

Let's also give them the freedom to decide for themselves who they would like for a partner in life. Let's not raise barriers to prevent our citizens from partaking equally in the rights guaranteed by our Constitution and legal benefits granted by our laws.

I urge my colleagues to vote against this narrow-minded legislation.

Mr. Neil Abercrombie, Democrat, of Hawaii:
Mr. Speaker, today I rise to speak against H.R. 3396, the Defense of Marriage Act. The title of the bill is puzzling. What are we defending marriage against: divorce, domestic violence, adultery? Can anyone name a single married couple whose union would be strengthened or

defended against harm by this legislation? With all the unresolved burning issues facing this institution, it is nothing short of incredible that we would be diverting time and energy away from questions like Medicare, the environment, and the economy on this matter.

Supporters of the bill point to what they claim is the danger of same-gender marriage. They say that if a court in Hawaii rules in favor of same-gender couples, other states will then have to give "full faith and credit" to the resulting marriages. I'm going to take this opportunity to concentrate on the traditions of our nation, in particular the rights of states and the Constitution of the United States. H.R. 3396 is an unnecessary intrusion into the state domain of family law. It tears at the fabric of our Constitution.

Historically, states have the primary authority to regulate marriage based upon the Tenth Amendment of the Constitution. The Supreme Court has supported this constitutional right. In *Ankenbrandt v. Richards*, 1992, the Court rules that "without exception, domestic relations has been a matter of state, not federal concern and control since the founding of the Republic."

It is also interesting to note that questions concerning the validity of an out-of-state marriage are generally resolved without reference to the "full faith and credit" clause of the US Constitution. States traditionally recognize out-of-state marriages unless they have statutes prohibiting such a union. For example, polygamy is illegal in all states, and in most states certain incestuous marriages are illegal too. States can declare an out-of-state marriage void if it is against the state's public policy or if entered into with the intent to evade the law of the state.

Congress has invoked the "full faith and credit" clause only five times since the founding of the republic. The three most recent instances have required each state to give child custody, child support, and protection orders of other states the same faith and credit it gives its own such orders. The Defense of Marriage Act differs in one critical aspect from the legislative enactment passed by the Congress under its "full faith and credit" power: H.R. 3396 permits sister states to give no effect to the laws of other states.

This is a novel and unconstitutional interpretation of the clause. According to a leading constitutional law scholar, Laurence H. Tribe, "the Constitution delegates to the United States no power to create categorical exceptions to the 'full faith and credit' clause."

The Supreme Court just recently struck down a Colorado law that targeted gays and lesbians in *Romer v. Evans*. This case suggests that the Supreme Court will rule legislation motivated by animus against gays and lesbians unconstitutional under the equal protection clause of the Fourteenth Amendment unless the legislative classification bears a rational relationship to a legitimate state purpose. In other words, since H.R. 3396 targets a group of people due to their—in the words of Gary Bauer of the Family Research Council—"dangerous lifestyle and behavior," it is likely to be struck down by the courts. There is no dire urgency or compelling public interest to pass this measure, which is not only unnecessary but also likely to be found unconstitutional by the Supreme Court.

In addition, I find it hard to believe how many of my colleagues can justify their support of H.R. 3396 when they are also cosponsors of H.R. 2270. At least thirty-seven members of the House are cosponsors of both bills. H.R. 2270 would require the Congress to specify the source of authority under the US Constitution for the enactment of laws. Where in Article I or anywhere else in the Constitution is the Congress given authority to write a national marriage law? Maybe the sponsors of both bills don't see the contradiction. Maybe they just don't care.

Many on the other side of the aisle have been vocal and unceasing in their support for reversing the flow of power away from Washington and back to the states. Well, the laws governing marriage are traditionally and constitutionally under the authority of the states. If there is any area of law to which states can lay a claim to exclusive authority, it is the field of family relations. How can someone reconcile being for states' rights while at the same time taking away a basic constitutional right given to states by the framers of our Constitution? I strongly encourage my colleagues to allow the states to continue exercising their constitutional rights and not fan the flames of intolerance. As William Eskridge, law professor at Georgetown University, simply stated, "The reasons to hesitate before adopting this legislation are conservative ones: federalism, original intent, and tradition."

Let us remember that the United States draws its strength from the enormous diversity to be found within the borders of our great nation. Vote against the Defense of Marriage Act.

REPRESENTATIVE GERRY STUDDS
(1937–2006)

Congressman Gerry Studds of Massachusetts was the first openly gay member of Congress, preceding Barney Frank by nearly a decade. He came out in the face of a scandal; he was censured in 1983 for having an inappropriate relationship with a seventeen-year-old page. He maintained the relationship was consensual and not something for which he felt shame, but chose not to fight censure, as it could have had repercussions for the page and his family.

In 1991, Congressman Studds began a relationship with Dean Hara, a Minnesota native who worked in Washington, DC. "We went to the same political and social dinners that all congressional couples are expected to attend. Yet, at that time, we would be the only openly gay couple there, and it was the first time it had happened," Hara recalled in an interview for this book. "Gerry would refer to it as the 'triumph of the routine.' By being out and living our lives we showed by example that we were like any other couple." By the mere fact of their presence and by making friendships, the couple slowly humanized gay people for conservative legislators.

Hara witnessed the contradiction between lawmakers' private opinions and how they felt they must vote when it came to gay rights. "I remember very specifically the night DOMA was voted on," Hara said. "It was the last year Gerry was going to be serving in Congress. We had been together for about five years. It was not unusual for me to meet Gerry on the Hill and eat in the members' dining room in order to have dinner with him. That night we made a specific point of dining there and when he went upstairs to make his statement, I went into the visitors' gallery. We both knew what was going to happen—that the horrendous, hateful legislation would be voted for, and that many of our friends, people we had socialized with, would vote against us."

Dean Hara and Gerry Studds married one week after gay marriage became legal in Massachusetts in May 2004. Studds died of a pulmonary embolism two years later. The cruel repercussions of DOMA meant that Hara didn't receive his husband's pension and health insurance—unlike all other spouses of a member of Congress, federal employee, or veteran. This was the case until June 2013, when the core provision of the Defense of Marriage Act was struck down. "I credit the Obama administration in how quickly they appear to be moving to implement the ruling. It would be a very different story if Obama wasn't in the White House," Hara said. "It sounds odd, but having the federal government recognize my marriage makes me feel that it's real."

In the decades after he was first outed, Congressman Studds emphasized the power of visibility and the power of being oneself. His comments testifying against the Defense of Marriage Act, with his spouse watching him from the visitors' gallery, are chilling and poignant.

66 *That Is Not True of My Partner* 99
Representative Gerry Studds
July 11, 1996

Mr. Speaker, first if I may make a legal observation, then a much more personal one. This bill has two brief sections: one purports to give states the rights to decline to recognize marriages in other states, and the other denies federal benefits to any state that makes such a decision. As has been said before, the first part is absolutely meaningless. Either under the Constitution states already have that right, in which case we do nothing, or they do not, in which case we cannot do anything because of the constitutional provisions; so much for the first part. We are then left with a federal provision that denies federal benefits for such a state that chooses to sanction a certain kind of marriage.

Mr. Speaker, I have served this House for twenty-four years; I have been elected twelve times, the last six times as an openly gay man. For the last six years, as many of the members of this House know, I have been in a relationship as loving, as caring, as committed, as nurtured and celebrated and sustained by our extended families as that of any member of this House. My partner Dean, whom a great many of you know and I think a great many of you love, is in a situation which no spouse of any member of this House is in. The same is true for my other openly gay colleagues. This is something that I don't think most people realize. The spouse of every member of this House is entitled to that member's health insurance even after that member dies, if he or she should predecease his or her spouse.

That is not true of my partner. The spouse of every member of this House knows that if he or she predeceases—is predeceased by their spouse, a member—that for the rest of their lives they have a pension long after, if they live after the death of a member of Congress. I have paid every single penny as much as any member of this House has for that pension, but my partner, should he survive me, is not entitled to one penny. I don't think that's fair, Mr. Speaker. I don't think most Americans think that is fair and that is really what the second section of this bill is about—to make sure that we continue that unfairness.

Did you know, for example, that if my partner Dean were terribly ill, that in a hospital, perhaps on death's door, that I could be refused the right to visit him in the hospital if a doctor did not approve of our relationship? Do you think that's fair? I don't think most Americans think that's fair. He can be fired solely because of his sexual orientation. He can be evicted from his home solely because of his sexual orientation. I don't think most Americans think that's fair. Mr. Speaker, not so long ago in this very country, women were denied the right to own property, and people of color, Mr. Speaker, were property. Not so very long ago, people of two races were not allowed to marry in many of the states of this country. Things change, Mr. Speaker, and they are changing now. We can embrace that change or we can resist that change, but thank God Almighty, as Dr. King would have said, we do not have the power to stop it. Thank you, Mr. Speaker.

REPRESENTATIVE BILL LIPPERT (1950–)

Before gay marriage, there were Vermont civil unions—an attempt to create a separate and somewhat equal version of marriage that would be accessible to people in same-sex relationships. Representative Bill Lippert, of Hinesburg, Vermont, was and is an instrumental figure in creating civil unions. In 2000, he was a lone out gay figure in the Vermont legislature. Lippert's words were spontaneous, coming in the eighth hour of a twelve-hour floor debate. In this interview (conducted by *We Do!* researcher Devorah Shubowitz on May 7, 2013), Representative Lippert reveals what prompted him to give personal testimony on the Vermont House floor on March 15, 2000.

Don't Tell Me What Love Is
Representative Bill Lippert
May 7, 2013

What is hard to remember now but was clear in 2000 was that gay marriage did not exist anywhere in the world. Delaware passed marriage equality today so eleven states plus Washington, DC, have some version of it, but in 2000, no one could have anticipated this progress. In December 1999, our Vermont Supreme Court unanimously ruled in *Baker v. State of Vermont* that same-sex couples had the constitutional right to all the rights, privileges, and responsibilities of Vermont's marriage statutes. But the court did not rule that marriage had to be granted. They said there could be the possibility of another legal structure, yet unnamed, that would grant these rights, privileges, and responsibilities. The plaintiffs in the case were three same-sex couples. The court left it to the Vermont legislature to determine whether marriage would be granted or whether a parallel legal structure would be created.

In 2000, I was the only gay member of the legislature and I was also the vice chair of the House Judiciary Committee, which was tasked with coming up with a response to the *Baker* decision. This placed me in a key position in these decisions. As a result of taking testimony in January, February, and the first half of March, the Judiciary Committee came to the conclusion that there was not sufficient support for gay marriage, but that there was unanimous support to create a parallel legal structure.

We were the first state to grant full legal recognition to gay couples. The national focus was intense. People traveled to Vermont from all over the country to make sure this would not happen. The attacks were hateful, so much so that members, including myself, received death threats. At the recommendation of security advisors, Governor Howard Dean wore a bulletproof vest when he campaigned that fall.

I understood that because of my unique position there would come a time when I would have the opportunity to speak. That opportunity came March 15, 2000, during the legislative debates. The House galleries were filled to the gills with people. People were sitting in all the hallways and all the floors. There was a candlelight vigil from supporters outside. We went into the debate not knowing if we had the votes to pass what we were calling "civil unions." We tried to create a phrase that stated that it was not a religious term but a dignified term.

There were only three word differences between Vermont state marriage laws and civil union laws: 1) civil union instead of marriage, 2) dissolution instead of divorce, 3) certify instead of solemnize. And civil union ceremonies, just like marriages, could be performed either by a justice of the peace or a minister. Also, for civil unions people have to be eighteen years of age; while people can marry at fourteen years of age with parental consent. The night before the vote I was so busy shoring up support, I remember suddenly thinking, *Oh My God, I am going to have to give a speech tomorrow.* One of my colleagues simply assured me, "Bill, don't worry, you already know what to say."

That night I recognized I had this unique opportunity to put a face on people in same-sex relationships, gay and lesbian people. During the debate I just kept jotting down notes as I thought of what I most wanted to have everyone hear. After eight hours of debate, the chairman said, "Bill, it is time for you to speak." It was the most profound moment of my life. I spoke extemporaneously. You could have heard a pin drop among hundreds and hundreds of people in the House Chamber.

I simply shared what I knew to be the truth about gay and lesbian people. I spoke about our goodness, what we endured—and specifically what we endured as a gay and lesbian community in Vermont. I spoke about what our allies endured. I watched committee members get attacked. I wanted to tell of what I had experienced to put a face on what had become the homophobic attacks on gay and lesbian people. Let's talk about who we are. Let's put a face on this. I knew without any level of doubt how incredibly loving and committed gay and lesbian relationships are. It has never been confusing to me about who we are and how courageous we have been. I wanted to affirm the reality that despite all the homophobic attacks that had been spewed against gay and lesbian people, they love and deeply care for one another in the face of historic prejudice.

I spoke about gay people who take care of each other as one was dying. Don't tell me what love is. I watched my friends hold their loved ones until their last moments. I talked about our relationships and how profoundly we loved one another in the face of that terrible epidemic.

More than a dozen of my colleagues were defeated because they voted for that civil union bill, but they were willing to risk their cherished political careers to support what they saw as a historic vote. It wasn't marriage in name but it was everything else. By 2009 the terminology shifted from *gay marriage* to *marriage equality*. I have chaired the Judiciary Committee since 2005, and in 2009, when we passed full marriage equality by overriding the governor's veto, there were five openly gay legislative members.

I came out in 1972 when I moved to Vermont. This was over thirty years later that I was speaking on the floor of the Vermont House. I never imagined in 1972 when I first came out that I would be doing this, let alone chair the House Judiciary Committee when we created marriage equality. I have had the privilege of living the gay rights struggle in Vermont.

I have been told that my speech changed people's votes that day. Allies in the face of persistent attacks stood with me and voted their conscience. Not one of these colleagues has regretted what they did. Their part in creating civil unions in 2000 was a highlight of their lives because it is so rare that you get the opportunity to make profound societal change. Over five thousand couples traveled to Vermont in the first several years to have a civil union ceremony and receive legal acknowledgment. Two women came from Malaysia to be joined in civil union. Two women from Idaho came because it was profoundly moving even though [their union] would not be recognized in their hometowns.

One of the governor's chief legal counsels said that as a woman she made it a rule not to cry in the state-house because that is what people expect of women, but she could not hold back. A few days after my speech I received an e-mail from South Africa from someone who said, "I woke up frustrated and discouraged with the world and your speech made me hopeful." That touched me deeply. Months after making that speech I was approached two to three times a day by GLBT individuals, family members, and friends to thank me. They told me how much it touched them. Some would pull out a copy of the speech and they would cry.

❝ *The Testimony* ❞
Bill Lippert
March 15, 2000

Thank you, Mr. Speaker. Representative Flory's strike-all amendment,[5] she indicates, is designed in part to remove "sexual activity" from the bill. At the same time, Representative Flory's strike-all amendment, unlike the bill of the House Judiciary Committee, fails to acknowledge that there has been discrimination and inequity toward gay and lesbian couples, currently and historically.

I think it's important to put a face on this. I think it's important to ask who it is that we're talking about; who it is that we've been discussing. I've had the privilege in my own life of coming to the process—through a struggle at times—the process of coming to identify myself as a gay man. I've had the privilege of developing a deep, devoted, loving, caring relationship with another man. I think it's very important as we listen, as we debate, and as we make decisions, that you understand what the reality is about gay and lesbian people, gay and lesbian couples.

Our mailboxes have been filled with letter after letter talking about abomination, talking about sinfulness, talking about Judgment Day coming soon. I'm here to tell you that gay and lesbian people and gay and lesbian couples deserve not only rights, they deserve to be celebrated. Our lives, in the midst of historic prejudice and

5. *A strike-all amendment removes all of the language of a bill and replaces it, potentially altering the intent of a bill but not its number.*

historic discrimination, are, to my view, in some ways, miracles.

Think what kind of relationship you would try to establish and how successful it would be to find a loving, committed partner in an environment where you have been barraged on a daily basis, from birth, saying you are sinful or wrong, that something is fundamentally flawed in your nature. It is, in truth, the goodness of gay and lesbian people and of gay and lesbian couples that is a triumph, is a *triumph*, against discrimination and prejudice. We are not a threat. We are not a threat to traditional marriage. We're not a threat to your communities. We are, in fact, an asset. We deserve to be welcomed, because in fact we are your neighbors; we are your friends; indeed, we are your family.

Numbers of people here have come up and talked to me privately about their gay brother, or lesbian sister, or their child, or their uncle. Part of those conversations are private, at times, because in fact prejudice and discrimination continues to exist in this society. Not everyone feels—even with the laws we have on our books now—not everyone feels able to say with openness and with pride, "Yes, my family member is a gay man or a lesbian woman."

We have made incredible progress in Vermont. And up until the last two and a half months, I would have said Vermont has more progress than any other state in this country. I have proudly said that. Our nondiscrimination laws, our hate crimes laws, our adoption laws, they all make us proud.

There remains afoot in Vermont prejudice against gay men and lesbians. In the last two and a half months I have seen and I have heard, I have been called names in this chamber, in this building, the likes of which I have never experienced in my life—my personal life or my political life. And, I've watched come true what I have always known to be true: that those who stand beside gay and lesbian people as their allies, as people who are going to stand up and say, "Yes, this is wrong," and "Yes, there should be rights," they get targeted too. Because for some people the hate runs that deep, the prejudice runs that far. I've watched while members of my committee have made brave political decisions to support equality for gay and lesbian people, for gay and lesbian couples, and rights for us, and I have watched them be attacked. I have stood there and listened while they have been threatened personally and politically, and I've had members of my committee say, "I couldn't sleep at night; I've had knots in my stomach." I wouldn't have wished this on any of them, but I am deeply appreciative of the work of my committee members who listened, who struggled, came to hard-reached decisions that it's the right thing to do.

Passing the bill that the House Judiciary Committee has brought forward will not end discrimination. It will not end prejudice. It will not end hate, but it will grant rights. We argue about whether they are civil rights or other rights, but I'll tell you this: they are rights that I don't have right now and most everyone else in this chamber does. There's something strange about sitting in the midst of a deliberative body that is trying to decide whether I and my fellow gay and lesbian Vermonters should get our rights now; should we wait a little longer; should we ask all the people whether or not we deserve to have those rights.

Who are we? We are committed, caring, loving individuals in a time when desire for greater commitment, greater love, greater fidelity is needed in our society, and I find it so ironic that rather than being embraced and welcomed we are seen as a threat. We are people, some of us who in recent times endured the scourge of a terrible epidemic, and even in the midst of that epidemic have reached out and formed relationships, cared for each other, holding each other, sometimes as death has arrived. Don't tell me about what a committed relationship is and isn't. I've watched my gay brothers care for each other deeply and my lesbian sisters nurse and care. There is no love and no commitment any greater than what I've seen, what I know.

Our relationships deserve every protection that our bill would grant. Our relationships deserve those rights, those protections. We don't need to study it any longer. We don't need to put it off and let someone else decide. We have a historic opportunity, and I ask us to put aside this amendment, which I trust is well intentioned, but I think flawed. I ask you to put aside the rest of these amendments as well. Let us move forward putting into law a bill that will set aside traditional marriage in order to meet the needs of those who somehow feel threatened, but will find a way through this thicket and will grant rights, will give a message to our community that it is time to take another piece of the hatred and the discrimination and the prejudice and remove it, and at the same time give an affirmation to our community about what it means to have full inclusivity, to embrace our neighbors, to affirm committed, loving relationships, and to affirm our common humanity.

Thank you, Mr. Speaker.

EVAN WOLFSON (1957–)

"Marriage is a language of love, equality, and inclusion," according to lawyer and activist Evan Wolfson, who has been called the "father of gay marriage." In 1983, while a student at Harvard Law School, Wolfson wrote his thesis on the constitutional merits of same-sex marriage. In addition to founding the Freedom to Marry organization, he wrote *Why Marriage Matters: America, Equality, and Gay People's Right to Marry* and has articulated that marriage is a "social statement, preeminently describing and defining a person's relationship and place in society." As a lawyer, he argued the *Boy Scouts of America v. Dale* before the Supreme Court in 2000, a case which hinged on the rights of a revered cultural institution to discriminate against gay people. He lost, but in 2013 the Boy Scouts of America removed their ban on gay scouts. On October 15, 2011, Wolfson married Cheng He in New York. In May 2012, he was awarded the Barnard Medal of Distinction during commencement, along with President Barack Obama.

Wolfson's 2004 Lavender Law keynote address to the National LGBT Bar Association in Minneapolis, Minnesota, presents some of his strategy to move the middle—that is, he advises proponents of gay marriage to resist fighting with the estimated one-third of the American population who actively oppose them or preaching to the one-third who are already on board. His arguments are designed to speak to the one-third who don't yet support marriage equality—but *could.*

> " *Marriage Equality and* "
> *Some Lessons for the Scary Work of Winning*
> Evan Wolfson
> *September 30, 2004*

One of the good things about my job is I have plenty of time on planes and trains in which to read.

Right now I'm reading the Library of America's anthology *Reporting Civil Rights.* In two volumes, they've collected the journalism of the 1940s, '50s, '60s, and '70s describing the blow-by-blow, the day-to-day, of what the struggles of those years felt and looked like . . . before those living through that moment knew how it was going to turn out.

Exhilarating, empowering, appalling, and scary.

That's what a civil rights moment feels like, when you are living through it—when it is uncertain and not yet wrapped in mythology or triumphant inevitablism.

This year our nation celebrated the fiftieth anniversary of *Brown v. Board of Education.* But what followed *Brown* was not the sincere and insincere embrace it gets today, but—in the words of the time: legislators in a swath of states declaring "massive resistance"; billboards saying, *Impeach Earl Warren*; members of Congress signing resolutions denouncing "activist judges"; and, of course, the marches, Freedom Rides, organizing summers, engagement, hard work, violence, legislation, transformations

. . . pretty much everything we today think of as the civil rights movement—all *after Brown*.

America is again in a civil rights moment, as same-sex couples, their loved ones, and non-gay allies struggle to end discrimination in marriage. A robust debate and numberless conversations are helping our nation (in Lincoln's words) "think anew" about how we are treating a group of families and fellow citizens among us. Today it is gay people, same-sex couples, LGBT individuals, and their loved ones and non-gay allies—we— who are contesting second-class citizenship, fighting for our loved ones and our country, seeking inclusion and equality—and it is scary as well as thrilling to see the changes and feel the movement.

How can we get through this moment of peril and secure the promise?

There are lessons we can learn from those who went before us . . . for we are not the first to have to fight for equality and inclusion. In fact, we are not the first to have to challenge discrimination even in *marriage*.

You see, marriage has always been a human rights battleground on which our nation has grappled with larger questions about what kind of country we are going to be: questions about the proper boundary between the individual and the government; questions about the equality of men and women; questions about the separation of church and state; questions about who gets to make important personal choices of life, liberty, and the pursuit of happiness.

As a nation, we have made changes in the institution of marriage, and fought over these questions of whether America is committed to both equality and freedom—in at least four major struggles in the past few decades:

- We ended the rules whereby the government, not couples, decided whether they should remain together when their marriages had failed or become abusive. Divorce transformed the so-called "traditional" definition of marriage from a union based on compulsion to what most of us think of marriage today—a union based on love, commitment, and the choice to be together and care for one another.
- We ended race restrictions on who could marry whom, based on the traditional "definition" of marriage, defended as part of God's plan, seemingly an intractable part of the social order of how things have to be.
- We ended the interference of the government in important personal decisions such as whether or not to procreate, whether or not to have sex without risking a pregnancy, whether or not to use contraceptives—even within marriage.
- And we ended the legal subordination of women in marriage—and thereby transforming the institution of marriage from a union based on domination and dynastic arrangement to what most of us think of it as today—a committed partnership of equals.

Yes, our nation has struggled with important questions on the human rights battlefield of marriage, and we are met on that battlefield once again . . .

As in any period of civil rights struggle, transformation will not come overnight. Rather, the classic American pattern of civil rights history is that our nation goes through a period of what I call in my book, *Why Marriage Matters*, "patchwork."

During such patchwork periods, we see some states move toward equality faster, while others resist and even regress, stampeded by pressure groups and pandering politicians into adding additional layers of discrimination before—eventually—buyer's remorse sets in and a national resolution comes.

So here we are in this civil rights patchwork. On the one hand, as the recent powerful and articulate rulings by courts in Washington and New York states demonstrated in the past few weeks, several states *are* advancing toward marriage equality, soon to join Massachusetts in ending discrimination and showing non-gay Americans the reality of families helped and no one hurt.

Meanwhile, on the other hand, as many as a dozen states targeted by opponents of equality as part of their own ideological campaign and for their political purposes could enact further *discriminatory* measures this year, compounding the second-class citizenship gay Americans already endure.

These opponents—anti-marriage-equality, yes, but also antigay, anti–women's equality, anti–civil rights, antichoice, and anti–separation of church and state—are throwing everything they have into this attack campaign because they know that if fair-minded people had a chance to hear the stories of real families and think it through, they would move toward fairness, as young people already have in their overwhelming support for marriage equality.

Most important, as Americans see the faces and hear the voices of couples in San Francisco; as they witness the families helped and no one hurt in Massachusetts and digest the reassuring way in which marriage equality is already finding acceptance there after just a few months; as they engage in conversations in every state and with many families, chats with people like us and non-gay allies—hearts and minds are opening and people are getting ready to accept, if not necessarily yet fully support, an end to discrimination in marriage . . .

In past chapters of civil rights history unfolding on the battlefield of marriage, this conversation and this patchwork of legal and political struggles would have proceeded in the first instance—and over quite some time—in the *states*, without federal interference or immediate national resolution.

That's because historically, domestic relations, including legal marriage, have under the American system of federalism been understood as principally (and almost entirely) the domain of the states.[6]

States worked out their discrepancies in who could marry whom under the general legal principles of comity, reflecting the value of national unity. The common-sense reality that it makes more sense to honor marriages than to destabilize them was embodied in the relevant spe-

---

6. Hisquierdo v. Hisquierdo, *439 US 572, 581 (1979)*. *"[I]nsofar as marriage is within temporal control, the States lay on the guiding hand." As the Supreme Court explained in* De Sylva v. Ballentine, *351 US 570, 580 (1956): "The scope of a federal right is, of course, a federal question, but that does not mean its content is not to be determined by state, rather than federal law . . . This is especially true when a statute deals with a familial relationship; there is no federal law of domestic relations, which is primarily a matter of state concern."*

cific legal principle, generally followed in all states—indeed, almost all jurisdictions around the world—that a marriage valid where celebrated will be respected elsewhere, even in places that would not themselves have performed that marriage.

States got to this logical result not primarily through legal compulsion, but through common sense—addressing the needs of the families and institutions (banks, businesses, employers, schools, etc.) before them. Eventually a national resolution came, grounded, again, in common sense, actual lived experience, and the nation's commitment to equality, constitutional guarantees, and expanding the circle of those included in the American dream.

But when it comes to constitutional principles such as equal protection—and, it now appears, even basic American safeguards such as checks-and-balances, the courts, and even federalism—antigay forces believe there should be a "gay exception" to the constitutions, to fairness, and to respect for families. Inserting the federal government into marriage for the first time in US history, our opponents federalized the question of marriage, prompting the passage of the so-called Defense of Marriage Act (DOMA) in 1996.

This federal antimarriage law creates an un-American caste system of first- and second-class marriages. If the federal government likes whom you marry, you get a vast array of legal and economic protections and recognition—ranging from Social Security and access to health care, to veterans benefits and immigration rights, to taxation and inheritance, and a myriad of others. (In a 2004 report, the Government Accountability Office, charged with auditing use of federal funds, identified 1,138 ways in which marriage implicates federal law.) Under so-called DOMA, if the federal government doesn't like whom you married, this typically automatic federal recognition and protection are withdrawn in all circumstances, no matter what the need.

The federal antimarriage law also purported to authorize states not to honor the lawful marriages from other states (provided those marriages were of same-sex couples)—in defiance of more than two hundred years of history in which, as I said, the states had largely worked out discrepancies in marriage laws among themselves under principles of comity and common sense, as well as the constitutional commitment to "full faith and credit."

When this radical law was first proposed, some of us spoke up immediately, saying it was unconstitutional—a violation of equal protection, the fundamental right to marry, federalist guarantees such as the "full faith and credit" clause, and limits on Congress's power. Ignoring our objections, our opponents pressed forward with their election-year attack.

Now they concede the unconstitutionality of the law they stampeded through just eight years ago, and are seeking an even more radical means of assuring gay people's second-class citizenship, this time through an assault on the US Constitution itself, as well as the constitutions of the states.

Because they do not trust the next generation, because they know they have no good arguments, no good reason for the harsh exclusion of same-sex couples from marriage, our opponents are desperate to tie the hands of all future generations, and as many states as possible, now.

This patchwork—and especially the next few weeks and months—will be difficult, painful, even ugly, and we will take hits. Indeed, we stand to take several hits in the states where our opponents have thrown antigay measures at us in their effort to deprive our fellow citizens of the information, the stories of gay couples to dispel stereotypes and refute right-wing lies, and the lived experience of the reality of marriage equality. While it is especially outrageous that the opponents of equality are using constitutions as the vehicles for this division and wave of attacks on American families, in the longer arc, their discrimination will not stand.

Here are a few basic lessons we can cling to in the difficult moments ahead, to help us keep our eye on the prize of the freedom to marry and full equality nationwide, a prize that shimmers within reach.

While we stand to lose several battles this year, we must remember that wins trump losses. Wins trump losses because each state that ends marriage discrimination allows fair-minded Americans to see and absorb the reality of families helped and no one hurt when the exclusion of same-sex couples from marriage ends. Nothing is more transformative, nothing moves the middle more than making it real, making it personal—and seeing other states join Canada and Massachusetts will be the engine of our victory.

Even where we cannot win a given battle, we can still engage and fight so as to at least *lose forward*, putting us in a better place for the inevitable next battle.

Now let me say a little more about this idea of "losing forward." After all, as someone most famous for the cases I lost, I've built an entire career on it.

Losing forward is a way that all of us can be part of this national campaign, no matter what our state. Even the more challenged states, the states with the greater uphill climb, the states where we are most outgunned and under attack—even those of us in the so-called "red states" still have a pivotal part in this national movement and can make a vital contribution.

In *every* state—even those where we cannot win the present battle, but fight so as to *lose forward*—we have the opportunity to enlist more support, build more coalitions, and make it possible for more candidates and non-gay opinion leaders to move toward fairness. All this contributes to the creation of the national climate of receptivity in which some states may cross the finish line before others, but everyone can be better positioned to catch the wave that will come back to every state in this national campaign.

Work on the ground in Georgia, for example, can get us a Bob Barr [the congressman who originally introduced the DOMA law] speaking out against the constitutional amendment, or make districts safe for African American leaders, or "surprising" voices to speak out in support of marriage equality. Work in Michigan—while perhaps not enough to win this round—can still help enlist prominent labor or corporate leaders to our cause. And working together, this national chorus will indeed swell, with some states further along and all participating, until all are free.

Wins trump losses. As long as we repel a federal constitutional amendment and continue to see some states move toward equality, beating back as many attacks as possible and enlisting more diverse voices in this conversation, we will win.

Now, the principal reason we are going to take hits this year and lose many, if not all, of the state attacks in November is because our opponents are cherry-picking their best targets and depriving the reachable middle of the chance to be reached. They have more of a head start, more money and more infrastructure through their megachurches and right-wing partners . . . and fear-mongering at a time of anxiety is easy to do. And, of course, historically, it is difficult to win civil rights *votes* at the early stage of a struggle.

But, to be honest, there is another reason, too, that we will not do well in most of these votes this year. Quite simply, our engagement, our campaigns in almost all of these states, are "too little, too late." We are starting too late to have enough time to sway people to fairness . . . and we are giving them too little to think about to guide them there. We have to avoid that error in the next wave of battles we face next year, which means, from California to Minnesota, from Wisconsin to Maine, starting *not* too late, but now, and by saying the word truly on people's minds, doing it right.

Put another way, the country right now is divided roughly in thirds. One-third supports equality for gay people, including the freedom to marry. Another third is not just adamantly against marriage for same-sex couples, but, indeed, opposes gay people and homosexuality, period. This group is against any measure of protection or recognition for lesbians and gay men, whether it be marriage or anything else.

And then there is the "middle" third—the reachable-but-not-yet-reached middle. These Americans are genuinely wrestling with this civil rights question and have divided impulses and feelings to sort through. How they frame the question for themselves brings them to different outcomes; their thinking is evolving as they grapple with the need for change to end discrimination in America.

What moves that middle?

To appeal to the better angels of their nature, we owe it to these friends, neighbors, and fellow citizens to help them understand the question of marriage equality through two truths:

Truth 1: Ending marriage discrimination is, first and foremost, about couples in love who have made a personal commitment to each other, who are doing the hard work of marriage in their lives, caring for one another and their kids, if any. (Think couples like Del Martin and Phyllis Lyon who've been together more than fifty years.) Now these people, having in truth made a personal commitment to each other, want and deserve a legal commitment.

Once the discussion has a human story, face, and voice, fair-minded people are ready to see through a second frame.

Truth 2: The exclusion of same-sex couples from marriage is discrimination; it is wrong, it is unfair to deny these couples and families marriage and its important tangible and intangible protections and responsibilities. America has had to make changes before to end discrimination and unfair treatment, and government should not be denying any American equality under the law.

When we see lopsided margins in these votes, it

means that under the gun in the first wave of electoral attacks, we have not as yet reached this middle. We can't be surprised *not* to win when in so many campaigns, and over so many opportunities to date (electoral campaigns and just month-to-month conversations), we have failed to give this middle third what they need to come out right.

When, in the name of "practicality" or advice from pollsters or political operatives, we fail to put forward compelling stories and explain the realities of what marriage equality does and does not mean, it costs us the one chance we have to do the heavy lifting that moves people. *We wind up not just not winning, but not even losing forward.*

By contrast, consider how we lost forward in California. In 2000, we took a hit, when the right-wing pushed the so-called Knight initiative and forced an early vote on marriage. We lost the vote, but because there had been some, though not enough, education about our families and the wrongs and costs of discrimination, polls showed that support for marriage equality actually rose after the election. And the very next year, activists pressed the legislature to enact a partnership law far broader than had been on the table in California before then. Our engagement over marriage continued, and within a couple years, legislators voted again, this time in support of an "all but marriage" bill, which takes effect this coming January. And California organizations and the national legal groups continue to engage for what we fully deserve—pursuing litigation in the California courts and legislation that would end marriage discrimination.

If we do our work right, making room for luck, we may see marriage in California, our largest state, as soon as next year. To go from a defeat in 2000 to partnership and "all but marriage" in 2004, with the possibility of marriage itself in 2005—that's called winning.

Remember, we have a secret weapon: death.

Or to put it more positively, we on the side of justice have generational momentum. Younger people overwhelmingly support ending this discrimination.

Americans are seeing more and more families like the Cheneys, and realizing, with increasing comfort, that we are part of the American family. The power of the marriage debate moves the center toward us, and as young people come into ascendancy, even the voting will change.

This is our opponents' last-ditch chance to pile up as many barricades as possible, but again, as long as we build that critical mass for equality and move the middle, we win.

Why is it so important that we *now* all redouble our outreach, our voices, our conversations in the vocabulary of marriage equality? In part because victory is within reach. In part because we can and must move that middle now to make room for that generational momentum and rise to fairness. In part because America is listening and allies are increasing. In part because this is our moment of greatest peril. And in part because the stakes are so great.

What is at stake in this civil rights and human rights moment?

If this struggle for same-sex couples' freedom to marry were "just" about gay people, it would be important—for gay men and lesbians, bisexuals, transgendered people, and our non-gay brothers and sisters are human beings, who share the aspirations for love, companionship, participation, equality, mutual caring and responsibility, protections for loved ones, and choice.

Yes, if this struggle were "just" about gay people, it would be important—but it is not "just" about gay people.

If this struggle were "just" about marriage, it would be important—for marriage is the gateway to a vast and otherwise largely inaccessible array of tangible and intangible protections and responsibilities, the vocabulary in which non-gay people talk about love, clarity, security, respect, family, intimacy, dedication, self-sacrifice, and equality. And the debate over marriage is the engine of other advances and the *inescapable* context in which we will be addressing all LGBT needs, the *inescapable* context in which we will be claiming our birthright of equality and enlarging possibilities for ourselves and others.

Yes, if this struggle were "just" about marriage, it would be important, but it is not "just" about marriage.

What is at stake in this struggle is what kind of country we are going to be.

Is America indeed to be a nation where we *all*, minorities as well as majorities, popular as well as unpopular, get to make important choices in our lives, not the government—or a land of liberty and justice only for some?

Is America indeed to be a nation that respects the separation of church and state, where government does not take sides on religious differences, but rather respects religious freedom while assuring equality under the law—or a land governed by one religious ideology imposed on all?

Is America to be a nation where two women who build a life together, maybe raise kids or tend to elderly parents, pay taxes, contribute to the community, care for one another, and even fight over who takes out the garbage, are free and equal—or a land where they can be told by their government that they are somehow lesser or incomplete or not whole because they do not have a man in their lives?

All of us, gay and non-gay, who share the vision of America as a nation that believes that all people have the right to be both different and equal, and that without real and sufficient justification, government may not compel people to give up their difference in order to be treated equally—all of us committed to holding America to that promise have a stake in this civil rights/human rights struggle for the freedom to marry.

And if we see every state, every methodology, every battle, every victory, and even every defeat as part of a *campaign*—and if we continue to enlist non-gay allies and voices in this campaign, transforming it into a truly organic *movement* for equality in the grand American tradition, we will move the middle; we will lose forward where necessary; we will empower the supportive; and we will win.

We *are* winning.

There is no marriage without engagement.

SENATOR TAMMY BALDWIN (1962–)

Fourteen years after being the first openly lesbian member of Congress, Tammy Baldwin became the first openly gay US senator (in 2012). In 1993, she called for her home state of Wisconsin to legalize gay marriage. That hasn't happened yet, but Baldwin's progressive record is a beacon for her colleagues. Her letter to leadership, printed below, reveals how far-reaching the issue of gay marriage is in American politics.

Dear President Obama
Senator Tammy Baldwin
February 2, 2010

Dear President Obama, Majority Leader Reid, Speaker Pelosi, Chairman Schumer, and Chairwoman Lofgren:

As members of the Congressional LGBT Equality Caucus, we are writing to express our strong support for a comprehensive immigration reform bill which would end discrimination against lesbian, gay, bisexual, and transgender (LGBT) binational families.

We urge Congress to include the Uniting American Families Act (H.R. 1024, S. 424) in any comprehensive immigration reform legislation.

Currently, US citizens and legal permanent residents

may sponsor their spouses (and other immediate family members) for immigration purposes. But, same-sex partners committed to spending their lives together are not recognized as "families" under US immigration law and thus do not have this same right. As a result, tens of thousands of binational families are either already living separately, face imminent separation, or have left the US entirely in order to remain together. This is unacceptable, and we believe comprehensive immigration reform legislation must include a strong family reunification component inclusive of LGBT families.

According to 2000 census data compiled by the Williams Institute, an estimated thirty-six thousand LGBT binational families are impacted by the inability to sponsor their partners for residency, and nearly half of those (47 percent) are raising children. Our existing, discriminatory immigration laws hurt not only those individuals, but their extended families, communities, and employers, as well. Not only would an inclusive family reunification provision strengthen American families, it would bolster the competitiveness of businesses in the US by allowing corporations to attract, employ, and retain the very best talent from across the globe. Indeed, the US lags behind nineteen countries that already recognize same-sex couples for immigration purposes, including the United Kingdom, Australia, Canada, France, and Germany.

In truth, no immigration reform bill can be called "comprehensive" unless it includes all Americans, including those who are LGBT. This is recognized in the Reuniting Families Act (H.R. 2709), which includes LGBT families in addressing the broader immigration problem of family unification.

We urge you to include LGBT binational families in comprehensive immigration reform legislation. No one should be forced to choose between the person they love and the country they call home. It is time that our immigration laws kept families together instead of tearing them apart.

Sincerely,
Tammy Baldwin, Congresswoman from Wisconsin
(cosigned by fifty-nine fellow members of Congress)

SENATOR JOHN KERRY (1943–)

John Kerry (D-MA) hails from a home state that was the first to legalize same-sex marriage (in 2004)— and brought to Congress both Barney Frank and Gerry Studds, the first two out gay congresspeople. Senator Kerry refused to sign the Defense of Marriage Act in 1996 and has long supported civil unions. Still, it wasn't until July 2011, after New York State passed marriage equality, that he went on record supporting gay marriage. According to an interview in the *Boston Globe*, Kerry acknowledged that his own Catholic church–fed fears that same-sex marriage would cause damage turned out to be unfounded. "I don't think it hurts the things I thought it would; lesson learned," he said. "You evolve with these things . . . The sort of concerns I had—that somehow it would have some impact on the quality of church teaching, or that I wasn't honoring that—I think is just not borne out by experience. Period."

Kerry's March 16, 2011 op-ed in *Bay Windows* lays out his argument against the Defense of Marriage Act and presaged his support, just months later, of full marriage equality.

" *Repeal the Defense of Marriage Act* "
Senator John Kerry
March 16, 2011

The so-called—wrongly named—Defense of Marrriage Act was both wrong and unconstitutional in 1996, and it's wrong and unconstitutional today.

It was legalized discrimination—not to mention an abuse of the Constitution for political purposes. My vote against it—which some predicted would cost me reelection in 1996—is among my proudest votes as a United States senator. But my job in 2011 isn't to feel good about my vote—or to boast that fifteen years later, I'm vindicated when at last an American president now agrees that DOMA is unconstitutional. No, my job—and our job together—is to work to undo the damage that DOMA has done in treating loving, committed couples like second-class citizens.

We know the impact of DOMA: every day, Americans are denied access to more than 1,100 federal benefits, including Social Security and numerous tax benefits— benefits that are derived from marriage and are available to every opposite-sex married couple.

That's why it's long overdue to put an end to this discrimination by putting an end to DOMA. We can do that with new legislation called the Respect for Marriage Act that would restore the rights of all lawfully married couples—gay or heterosexual. I am committed to DOMA's repeal as quickly as possible and I believe we can make that happen through the Respect for Marriage Act.

Thankfully, DOMA is already under assault in the federal courts, one of which—here in Massachusetts— struck down a key portion of the law as unconstitutional. In a powerfully worded ruling last summer, Judge Joseph Tauro of the federal district court in Boston decimated the argument that DOMA is a legitimate effort to preserve the existing social order to buy time to digest the controversial idea of same-sex marriage. "If the Constitution means anything, it does at the very least mean that the Constitution will not abide a bare congressional desire to harm a politically, unpopular group," Judge Tauro wrote. He got it exactly right. But the wheels of justice can move way too slowly, as we all know. Congress doesn't have to wait for the courts to right the wrongs. We can do it legislatively—usually faster than the judicial system allows—and that is the aim of the Respect for Marriage Act.

The Respect for Marriage Act repeals key sections of DOMA—and the immediate effect of doing away with those provisions would be that same-sex couples and their families would be eligible for important federal benefits and protections, such as family and medical leave, Social Security spousal and survivors' benefits, and filing joint federal tax returns.

What it would *not* do is require states that have not yet enacted legal protections for same-sex couples to recognize any marriage. But it would guarantee that the federal government would stop discriminating against same-sex couples who were legally married in one state regardless of the state laws in another state where they may choose to live. That way, we can avoid a ridiculous situation in which, for example, a same-sex couple is married in Massachusetts, with federal rights, but loses them when a job transfer brings them to a state that does not recognize their marriage. This is an important feature because the system of federal benefits has always been based upon marriage.

On these issues, I believe America is moving in the right direction. Five states now allow same-sex couples to marry; several others recognize civil unions. Moreover, Congress finally repealed the "Don't Ask, Don't Tell" policy that forced gay service members to live a lie in order to serve their country. The next step is to relegate DOMA to the dustbin of history.

PART III

FROM SEEING CHANGE TO SEA CHANGE

MAYOR GAVIN NEWSOM (1967–)

U sually homophobic bigotry is just accepted, but sometimes, as in the case of the Stonewall riots, it inspires historic change. Similarly, in late 2003, the Supreme Court of Massachusetts found in *Goodridge v. Department of Public Health* that it was against that state's constitution to allow only heterosexual couples to marry. In his 2004 inaugural address, President George W. Bush reacted. He criticized the decision of "activist judges" and proclaimed, "If judges insist on forcing their arbitrary will upon the people, the only alternative left to the people would be the constitutional process. Our nation must defend the sanctity of marriage."

Gavin Newsom, then the thirty-seven-year-old mayor of San Francisco (and currently lieutenant governor of California), was in the audience when President Bush called for a federal marriage amendment. On February 12, a few weeks later, Mayor Newsom directed the city clerk to begin issuing marriage licenses to same-sex couples. More than four thousand marriage licenses were issued from February 12 until March 11, when the California Supreme Court issued a stay, pending court review of the legality of Newsom's actions.

After the California Supreme Court agreed that banning same-sex marriage was not compatible with the state constitution, a voter referendum in 2008 known as Proposition 8 again outlawed the marriages. On June

26, 2013, a 5–4 US Supreme Court majority ruled that the proponents of Proposition 8 had no standing to continue appeals to defy the state's constitution—and effectively wiped away an earlier court of appeals ruling in the proposition's favor. In these excerpts from an interview on CNN, Newsom lays out the justification for his historic actions.

Late Edition with Wolf Blitzer
Gavin Newsom
February 22, 2004

"It is time for the city to stop traveling down this dangerous path of ignoring the rule of law."

Wolf Blitzer: [That was] California Governor Arnold Schwarzenegger warning the city of San Francisco about its decision to allow same-sex marriages.

Gavin Newsom: I don't believe I'm breaking the law. I believe what we're doing is affirming the constitution of the state of California and its equal protection clause, which says I don't have a right to discriminate. And just forty-five days ago, I took an oath of office to bear truth, faith, and allegiance to the constitution of the state of California, and there is nothing in that constitution that says that I have the right to discriminate against people on any basis. And I simply won't do that.

WB: As you know, California Proposition 22 that passed in 2000, 61 percent to 39 percent, says flatly: *Only marriage* *between a man and a woman is valid or recognized in California.* That, I believe, is the law of the land, isn't it?

GN: Well, we're in the courts right now on just that question. I don't believe that it's consistent, Prop 22, with the constitution of the state of California. Not only do I not believe that, but the city attorney's office in San Francisco feels very strongly about that as well.

We've been in hearings four times in front of two judges, and in neither case, or rather in any of those proceedings, have there been any suggestion that what we're doing is going to cause irreparable harm, irreparable damage, and that the question of whether or not we're doing what is constitutionally appropriate will be heard through a court of law in a process that's under way. And I look forward to that discussion and debate.

WB: But why did you go ahead and effectively change the rules of the game without going to court first, just simply unilaterally saying, "Go ahead, same-sex couples, you can get marriage licenses."

A lot of people, including many gay leaders, suggested that you simply went about it the wrong way, by unilaterally deciding what is legal and what is illegal.

GN: Well, Wolf, I wanted to stand on principle. I feel very strongly that the oath of office I took—and again, maybe it's just fresh in my mind, just forty-five days ago—to bear truth, faith, and allegiance to this constitution, I think I have an obligation not to discriminate against people.

I wanted to put a human face on it. I mean, we're

dealing with people's lives here. The first couple that was married in San Francisco had been together fifty-one years. To me, that's an affirmation of marriage. It's an affirmation of my own marriage with my wife. I feel very strongly that you can't discriminate in theory.

We've got to see the human lives; we've got to connect this discussion and debate with human beings and their families, so we can understand what we're doing is wrong and inconsistent with the values I think this country holds dear . . . It's about human beings. It's about human dignity. It's about advancing and affirming marriage in a unique bond and relationship. It's about, I think, holding truth, faith, and allegiance to the constitution. I feel very strongly this is consistent. And I say that, Wolf, with some consideration. I mean, the fact is, every time these debates come to the supreme courts in states across this country, the constitution affirms the decisions like the decision that I've taken. Not least of which, obviously, in Massachusetts, but Hawaii and Alaska.

I think we're on firm legal footing and legal grounds, and certainly I believe very strongly and passionately we're on the right moral ground. I do not believe in advancing separate-but-unequal status. I do not believe in advancing discrimination.

I've got an obligation to stand on principle and not abdicate for another day, not wait another month. These were the same debates we were having on interracial relationships just a few decades ago, where blacks couldn't marry whites. We need, I think, to stand up on principle, and I think San Francisco's done just that . . .

The system is working. The system was set up for

just this kind of decision and this kind of action. And it's working, it's advancing through those courts, not in front of one judge, but two different judges, in three separate hearings of the lower court, and one was rejected at the appellate court. We have a date set, a date certain. We're going to discuss the constitutional questions.

But I will not abdicate and step back and say what we were doing ten, fifteen days ago, before this action, is appropriate. I do not believe it's appropriate for me, as mayor of San Francisco, to discriminate against people. And if that means my political career ends, so be it.

Guys like me come and go, but there are certain principles that I hold dear, and the principle of nondiscrimination, of advancing human rights and civil rights, affirming marriage, affirming relationships and families, like we've done for three thousand–plus couples, that's significant, that's purposeful. And I believe very strongly what we're doing is appropriate.

WB: Congressman Barney Frank of Massachusetts, who is homosexual himself, openly homosexual for a long time, knows a great deal about this issue. He said this the other day. He said, "If we go forward in Massachusetts and get same-sex marriage on the books, it's going to be binding and incontestable. When you're in a real struggle, San Francisco making a symbolic point becomes a diversion."

Do you understand the criticism he's leveling against you?

GN: Yes, and I have great respect for Barney Frank. I

don't think it's symbolic to Phyllis Lyon and Del Martin, a relationship of five decades. I think it's very significant for them. If people had the opportunity, as I have, to witness these kinds of bonds, to witness these kinds of unions, to see life and marriage affirmed, to see children weeping because finally their parents have the same kind of rights that are extended to my relationship with my wife, it is real, it's tangible now. It's not in the courts or some theory. It's being practiced.

These are the same discussions and same debates we were having between 1948 and 1967, when California got the ball rolling on interracial relationships and marriages. It's exactly the same debate. We need to advance the dignity of humanity and the dignity of our commonality by advancing the bonds of marriage, and that's all we're doing here in San Francisco.

WB: Well, what happens if in March, maybe even earlier, the courts rule against what you've done? Some 3,200 couples already have been married. They would be in legal limbo. Aren't you toying with their feelings, their emotions, right now?

GN: I frankly think politicians have been toying with their emotions for decades by abdicating responsibility, by saying one thing privately and saying another publicly, by sitting back and waiting for tomorrow, waiting for the next round of debates, waiting for the next state to do something.

You've got to stand up on principle. Every single person that came in to City Hall to get a marriage knew exactly what they were doing. People from all over the world, literally, from about two dozen states, came to San Francisco knowing exactly the challenges ahead, because they've lived it, they've lived the discrimination, they've lived the separate-but-unequal status, and they're fed up, and they came in to celebrate and affirm life and marriage. And that, to me, is an extraordinary thing. And I, as a married man, feel my marriage was affirmed in turn.

WB: City Hall has been open almost around the clock over the past ten, eleven days, but now you're changing the process. Starting tomorrow, people will be able to get marriage licenses, same-sex couples, by appointment only. That will limit it to, what, fifty or sixty couples a day? Why the change?

GN: Well, I'll be honest with you. We have human beings doing great work, they're exhausted at City Hall. The whole point of this was, it's the right thing to do. We also have other things to do, and City Hall just simply doesn't have the capacity. I had two hundred–plus volunteers. Our assessors have done an incredible job. They're exhausted.

We still want to afford this right and privilege, and we want to extend these obligations of marriage to same-sex couples, so we're not going to stop. But we don't have the capacity to continue at the pace we've been at over the last ten days.

WB: Let's talk about the politics of your decision. There's a CNN/USA Today/Gallup poll today that came out this week. "Should gay marriages be recognized as legally valid?" Thirty-two percent said yes; 64 percent said no.

Some Democrats fear what you're doing is giving the Republicans, to a certain degree, an opening right now, especially President Bush, who's raising the specter of a constitutional amendment, you're giving them an opening in the political world.

GN: Yes, but let's be honest here. In the State of the Union, the president made this an issue. He decided to take on this issue in the State of the Union. This was hardly something unique to San Francisco. We're reacting to the president's decision to use this as a wedge issue to divide people.

I think what he's doing is wrong. It's hurtful. And I hope he reconsiders the notion of advancing a constitutional amendment. And I hope that the Republican Party recognizes how divisive this could be across this nation.

No, we're simply reacting to the president, and we're reacting to a train that had left many, many months ago. And I think it's inappropriate and unfortunate that he's decided to use this to advance a political agenda, which only seems to me, when you're doing something in the State of the Union—and I had the privilege of being there at the State of the Union, to listen to his words firsthand—that he's doing it in a way that, of course, associates the statements with a political agenda in order to get reelected. I just don't think that's right.

WB: One outspoken opponent of your decision, Randy Thomasson, the founder of Campaign for California, which opposes gay marriage, was quoted in *Newsweek* saying, "Gavin Newsom is a renegade. And the word *equality* is being misused to rob all the sacred things of their uniqueness. What's next—legalized heroin? Prostitution? Polygamy? Incest?"

GN: Yes. I mean, you know, I mean, stale rhetoric. Stale rhetoric. Divisive rhetoric. Absurd.

It's exactly the same kind of rhetoric that was used against blacks marrying whites in the '60s. The same kind of rhetoric was used when they made comments about Catholics being able to marry Protestants at the turn of the century. I imagine it was the same rhetoric some people used when they said, "What do these women want? Why do they want to vote in this country?"

No, I'm a student of history. I've heard this before, the "What next?" arguments. And to me, they fall flat on their face.

And, Wolf, just one thing. If I wait for the polls in this country to turn around, we're never going to change the order of things in this country. I mean, when *Loving v. Virginia*, which finally established the fact that interracial marriages in 1967 can exist in every state in the nation, and those sixteen states that were holding out couldn't hold out, the polls didn't suggest it was a good decision.

If you wait for public opinion, nothing changes. Polls, to me, don't matter. Principles matter. That's the foundation of this country—people standing up on principle and moving the agenda forward and bringing people together. Focus on our common humanity and decency. That's what makes a good country a great country, by affirming people in their unique bond and relation to one another.

PROMINENT POLITICIANS
DARE TO EVOLVE

By the early 2000s, a host of prominent politicians began to change their position on gay marriage, usually because a gay family member came out, transforming an abstract political issue into one that is urgently personal. The leaders quoted below hold a wide range of political philosophies, but each has come to see gay marriage as a goal that upholds some cherished and sometimes even conservative American values.[7]

Former Vice President Dick Cheney
During his two terms as George W. Bush's vice president, Cheney changed. Initially, although his daughter Mary, a lesbian, was out, his wife commented to Cokie Roberts that "Mary has never declared" she was a lesbian—intimating that it was just a rumor. By 2002, Cheney was on record saying that he believed same-sex marriage should be left to the states to decide. He noted,

---

7. *Sources for these and other political figures were gathered from Andrew Kaczynski, "11 Politicians Who Changed Their Minds on Gay Marriage," BuzzFeed Politics, May 9, 2012, http://www.buzzfeed.com/ andrewkaczynski/11-politicans-who-changed-their-minds-on-gay-marri; and Alisa Wiersema, "High-Profile Politicians Who Changed Their Positions on Gay Marriage," ABC News, March 15, 2013, http://abcnews.go.com/Politics/ high-profile-politicians-changed-positions-gay-marriage/story?id=18740293#. UYHLcUofySo. The quotes from Barack Obama were originally collected by Mackenzie Weinger, "Evolve: Obama Gay Marriage Quotes," Politico, May 9, 2012, http://www.politico.com/news/stories/0512/76109.html.*

however, that Bush endorsed a constitutional amendment preventing the states from recognizing such marriages, banning civil unions and domestic partnership benefits, and that it was the president who set policy. By the 2004 election, his daughter served as director of vice presidential operations and Cheney often responded to questions about gay rights and gay marriage that "I think freedom means freedom for everyone."

> "As many of you know, one of my daughters is gay, and something that we have lived with for a long time in our family. I think people ought to be free to enter into any kind of union they wish, any kind of arrangement they wish. The question of whether or not there ought to be a federal statute that governs this, I don't support. I do believe that historically the way marriage has been regulated is at the state level, this has always been a state issue, and I think that is the way that ought to be handled today—that is, on a state-by-state basis, different states will make different decisions. But I don't have any problem with [gay marriage]. I think people ought to get a shot at that."
>
> —Dick Cheney, National Press Club, Gerald R. Ford Foundation Journalism Awards, Washington, DC, June 1, 2009

Vice President Joe Biden

Although he voted for the Defense of Marriage Act in 1996, Vice President Biden was able to use his mix of off-the-cuff genuineness and ability to weather gaffes to push the Obama administration on the issue of gay marriage. This exchange on *Meet the Press* from May 6, 2012, may have changed history.

David Gregory: *You raise social policy. I'm curious. You know, the president has said that his views on gay marriage, on same-sex marriage, have evolved. But he's opposed to it. You're opposed to it. Have your views—evolved?*

Vice President Joe Biden: *Look, I just think that the good news is that as more and more Americans become to understand what this is all about is a simple proposition. Who do you love? Who do you love and will you be loyal to the person you love? And that's what people are finding out, is what—what all marriages, at their root, are about. Whether they're marriages of lesbians or gay men or heterosexuals.*

DG: *Is that what you believe now?*

JB: *That's what I believe.*

DG: *And you're comfortable with same-sex marriage now?*

JB: *I—I—look, I am vice president of the United States of America. The president sets the policy. I am absolutely comfortable with the fact that men marrying men, women marrying women, and heterosexual men and women marrying one another are entitled to the same exact rights, all the civil rights, all the civil liberties. And quite frankly, I don't see much of a distinction beyond that.*

DG: *In a second term, will this administration come out behind same-sex marriage, the institution of marriage?*

JB: *Well, I can't speak to that. I don't know the answer to that. But I can tell you—*

DG: *It sounds like you'd like to see it happen. If that's what the president would get—*

JB: *Well, the president continues to fight, whether it's "Don't Ask, Don't Tell" or whether it is making sure, across the board, that you cannot discriminate. Look at the executive orders he's put in place. Any hospital that gets federal funding, which is almost all of them, they can't deny a partner from being able to have access to their partner who's ill or making the call on whether or not they . . . This is evolving.*

And by the way, my measure, David, and I take a look at when things really begin to change, is when the social culture changes. I think Will *and* Grace *probably did more to educate the American public than almost anything anybody's ever done so far. And I think people fear that which is different. Now they're beginning to understand.*

I was speaking to a group of gay leaders in Los Angeles two weeks ago. And one gentleman looked at me in the question period and said, "Let me ask you, how do you feel about us?" And I had just walked into the back door of this gay couple and they're with their two adopted children. And I turned to the man who owned the house. I said, "What did I do when I walked in?" He said, "You walked right to my children. They were seven and five, giving you flowers." And I said, "I wish every American could see the look of love those kids had in their eyes for you guys. And they wouldn't have any doubt about what this is about.

Senator Rob Portman (R-Ohio)

Although Senator Portman had earlier stated that marriage was a sacred bond between a man and a woman, learning that his son was gay offered him an opportunity to rethink what gay marriage means.

"I have come to believe that if two people are prepared to make a lifetime commitment to love and care for each other in good times and in bad, the government shouldn't deny them the opportunity to get married . . . We conservatives believe in personal liberty and minimal government interference in people's lives. We also consider the family unit to be the fundamental building block of society. We should encourage people to make long-term commitments to each other and build families, so as to foster strong, stable communities and promote personal responsibility. One way to look at it is that gay couples' desire to marry doesn't amount to a threat but rather a tribute to marriage, and a potential source of renewed strength for the institution."

—Senator Rob Portman, editorial,
Columbus Dispatch, March 15, 2013

Former Vice President Al Gore

During his run for president in 2000, Gore acknowledged supporting the Defense of Marriage Act. At an October 11 presidential debate at Wake Forest University, Vice President Gore attempted to distinguish himself from the positions of his opponent, George W. Bush, by announcing his desire to "find a way to allow some kind of civic unions." In January 2008, safely out of office, Al Gore used Current TV to post a one-minute video supporting same-sex marriage:

"I think it is wrong for the government to discriminate against individuals because of their sexual orientation. I think gay men and women ought to have the same rights as heterosexual men and women to make contracts and have hospital visiting rights and join together in marriage. I don't understand why it is considered by some people to be a threat to heterosexual marriage to allow it by gays and lesbians. Shouldn't we be promoting the kind of faithfulness and loyalty to one's partner regardless of sexual orientation? Because if you don't do that then you are promoting promiscuity and all the problems resulting from promiscuity. The loyalty and love the two people feel for each other should be encouraged. It should not be prevented by any form of discrimination in the law."

Senator Tom Harkin (D-Iowa)

On April 3, 2009, Iowa became the third state to legalize same-sex marriage. The state's long-time progressive senator Tom Harkin remarked:

"We all grow as we get older and we learn things and we become more sensitive to people and people's lives . . . And I guess I'm at the point that, you know—I'm to that point of live and let live. There's always going to be some who feel that they have to push this issue, and for whatever reason, they're going to try to push it and try to divide people up, but they're on the losing end. They're on the losing end of history."

Former President Jimmy Carter

As a born-again Christian and someone who could boast sixty-five-plus years of marriage, President Carter had a certain special authority when he announced in March 2012 during a book tour for *NIV Lessons from Life Bible: Personal Reflections with Jimmy Carter* that he supported same-sex marriage.

> *"Homosexuality was well known in the ancient world, well before Christ was born, and Jesus never said a word about homosexuality. In all of His teachings about multiple things—He never said that gay people should be condemned. I personally think it is very fine for gay people to be married in civil ceremonies. I draw the line, maybe arbitrarily, in requiring by law that churches must marry people. I'm a Baptist, and I believe that each congregation is autonomous and can govern its own affairs. So if a local Baptist church wants to accept gay members on an equal basis, which my church does, by the way, then that is fine. If a church decides not to, then government laws shouldn't require them to."*

Former Secretary of State Hillary Clinton

Hillary Clinton's marriage, like that of many heterosexual politicians, has faced (and withstood) far greater threats than gay marriage could ever pose. In 2013, she came out with the following message of support, contributing to a groundswell of Democratic politicians trumpeting marriage equality as the civil rights struggle of our era—and provoking further speculation that Clinton would run for president in 2016.

> *"LGBT Americans are our colleagues, our teachers, our soldiers, our friends, our loved ones, and they are full and equal citizens and deserve the rights of citizenship. That in-*

cludes marriage . . . I support it personally, and as matter of policy and law.

"Like so many others, my personal views have been shaped over time by people I have known and loved, by my experience representing our nation on the world stage, my devotion to law and human rights and the guiding principles of my faith. Marriage, after all, is a fundamental building block of our society. A great joy, and yes, a great responsibility.

"A few years ago, Bill and I celebrated as our own daughter married the love of her life. I wish every parent that same joy. To deny the opportunity to our own daughters and sons solely on the basis of who they are and who they love is to deny them the chance to live up to their own God-given potential.

"For those of us who lived through the long years of the civil rights and women's rights movements, the speed with which more and more people have come to embrace the dignity and equality of LGBT Americans has been breathtaking and inspiring. We see it all around us, every day, in major cultural statements and in quiet family moments. But the journey is far from over, and therefore we must keep working to make our country freer and fairer."

—Hillary Clinton, Human Rights
Campaign Video, March 2013

President Barack Obama

More so than with any previous president, Barack Obama's attempt to support gay people while also defending the idea that marriage is between a man and a woman was painful to witness. President Obama, both through his insightful first memoir and his historic role as the first African American leader of the free world, has appeared attuned to the dehumanizing effects of bigotry by any name. His backtracking on the issue over the years is both shocking and a good reminder of how far we've come in a short time when it comes to human rights for gay people.

"I favor legalizing same-sex marriages, and would fight efforts to prohibit such marriages."

—1996

"Undecided."

—1998, in response to an *Outlines* questionnaire asking, "Do you favor legalizing same-sex marriage?"

"I am a fierce supporter of domestic partnership and civil union laws. I am not a supporter of gay marriage as it has been thrown about, primarily just as a strategic issue. I think that marriage, in the minds of a lot of voters, has a religious connotation. I know that's true in the African American community, for example. And if you asked people, 'Should gay and lesbian people have the same rights to transfer property, and visit hospitals, and et cetera,' they would say, 'Absolutely.' And then if you talk about, 'Should they get married?' then suddenly . . . "

—2004

"I was reminded that it is my obligation not only as an elected official in a pluralistic society, but also as a Christian, to remain open to the possibility that my unwillingness to support gay marriage is misguided."

—2006

"*The government has to treat all citizens equally. I am a strong supporter not of a weak version of civil unions, but of a strong version, in which the rights that are conferred at the federal level to persons who are part of the same-sex union are compatible. When it comes to federal rights, the over 1,100 rights that right now are not being given to same-sex couples, I think that's unacceptable.*"

—2007

"*I believe that marriage is the union between a man and a woman. Now, for me as a Christian—for me—for me as a Christian, it is also a sacred union. God's in the mix.*"

—2008

"*I believe marriage is between a man and a woman. I am not in favor of gay marriage. But when you start playing around with constitutions, just to prohibit somebody who cares about another person, it just seems to me that's not what America's about.*"

—2008

"*I've called on Congress to repeal the so-called Defense of Marriage Act to help end discrimination against same-sex couples in this country. Now, I want to add we have a duty to uphold existing law, but I believe we must do so in a way that does not exacerbate old divides. And fulfilling this duty in upholding the law in no way lessens my commitment to reversing this law. I've made that clear.*"

—2009

"*I have been to this point unwilling to sign on to same-sex marriage primarily because of my understandings of the traditional definitions of marriage. But I also think you're right that attitudes evolve, including mine."*

—2010

"Every single American—gay, straight, lesbian, bisexual, transgender—every single American deserves to be treated equally in the eyes of the law and in the eyes of our society. It's a pretty simple proposition."

—2011

"I've just concluded that for me personally it is important for me to go ahead and affirm that I think same-sex couples should be able to get married."

—2012

"Our journey is not complete until our gay brothers and sisters are treated like anyone else under the law. For if we are truly created equal, then surely the love we commit to one another must be equal as well."

—2013, inauguration speech

REPRESENTATIVE BOB BARR (1948–)

When Congressman Bob Barr (R-Georgia, 1995–2003) authored and introduced the Defense of Marriage Act in May 1996, he was one of the most conservative—and frequently divorced—lawmakers in Congress. His inability to defend his own marriages was the least of his contradictions. He was a small-government, anti-regulation conservative advocating that the federal government be in the marriage business. Fifteen years later, out of office and perhaps with time to think, he delivered a major renunciation of DOMA and "Don't Ask, Don't Tell." The audience? The Log Cabin Republicans, the most established group of gay rights lobbyists who are also small-government conservatives.

In his 2011 speech, Barr repeatedly argued that almost any law that expands government should be opposed, on the grounds that government is in essential conflict with individual liberty. "Some degree of government is necessary," he stated. But "any degree of government that is more than necessary itself intrudes on these rights, and should (must) be opposed, [including] those laws limiting personal choices and relationships that do not harm others."

Taking a dim view of licensing requirements for any activities, Barr asked the crowd, "Why do individuals need the government's permission to marry?" and noted a cumbersome morass of laws and regulations around marriage that confer "more than 1,100 rights, duties, and entitlements granted only with the state's permission." Our Bill of Rights protects "the fundamental freedom to possess and act on one's own private beliefs and desires; to live one's life as one wishes. This reflects the fundamental right to privacy . . ." Speaking of such fundamentals, Barr (a lawyer) noted that the Supreme Court consistently "held that 'marriage' is a fundamental right" in *Loving v. Virginia* (which struck down bans on interracial marriage in 1967), *Zablocki v. Redhail* (1978), and *Turner v. Safley* (which, in 1987, ruled that prisoners have the right to marry). Barr quoted the court in *Zablocki v. Redhail*, noting:

> [T]he right to marry is of fundamental importance for all individuals. It is not surprising that the decision to marry has been placed on the same level of importance as decisions relating to procreation, childbirth, child rearing, and family relationships. As the facts of this case illustrate, it would make little sense to recognize a right of privacy with respect to other matters of family life and not with respect to the decision to enter the relationship that is the foundation of the family in our society.

Barr, who in 2013 was running for Congress again, concluded that ". . . using the collective power of the state to do what individuals cannot do—impose the will of one group of people on another set of people—is truly immoral."

MAYOR MICHAEL R. BLOOMBERG (1942–)

M ayor Bloomberg first came out in support of gay marriage at a Chinatown press conference in February 2005, where he said, simply, "I think anybody should be allowed to marry anybody." His endorsement came six years before same-sex marriage passed the New York legislature. Mayor Bloomberg's commitment to civil rights for gay people and marriage equality has stayed strong and practical over the years, as when he remarked in July 2012, "Marriage equality has made our city more open, inclusive, and free—and it has also helped to create jobs and support our economy." The following are Mayor Bloomberg's most comprehensive remarks about gay marriage as a civil rights struggle of this era, prepared for delivery at the Cooper Union for the Advancement of Science and Art.

66 99

The Urgent Need
for Marriage Equality
Mayor Michael R. Bloomburg
May 26, 2011

I think it's fair to say that no institute of higher learning has had a more profound impact on the course of American history than Cooper Union. By opening the doors of its Great Hall to Abraham Lincoln, Frederick

Douglass, Susan B. Anthony, Elizabeth Cady Stanton, and so many other pioneering leaders, and by hosting the founding of the NAACP, Cooper Union has helped push American freedom ever higher, and ever wider.

Today, we gather in this innovative and striking new academic building—a symbol of how Cooper Union has always looked forward and always championed progress. We gather—in the tradition of those who came before us—to discuss a momentous question before our nation and our great State of New York: should government permit men and women of the same sex to marry?

It is a question that cuts to the core of who we are as a country—and as a city. It is a question that deserves to be answered here in New York—which was the birthplace of the gay rights movement, more than forty years ago. And it is a question that requires us to step back from the platitudes and partisanship of the everyday political debate and consider the principles that must lead us forward.

The principles that have guided our nation since its founding—freedom, liberty, equality—are the principles that have animated generations of Americans to expand opportunity to an ever-wider circle of our citizenry. At our founding, African Americans were held in bondage. Catholics in New York could not hold office. Those without property could not vote. Women could not vote or hold office. And homosexuality was, in some places, a crime punishable by death.

One by one, over many long years, the legal prohibitions to freedom and equality were overcome: some on the battlefield, some at the statehouse, and some in the courthouse. Throughout our history, each and every generation has expanded upon the freedoms won by their parents and grandparents. Each and every generation has removed some barrier to full participation in the American dream. Each and every generation has helped our country take another step on the road to a more perfect union for all our citizens. That is the arc of American history. That is the march of freedom. That is the journey that we must never stop traveling. And that is the reason we are here today.

The next great barrier standing before our generation is the prohibition on marriage for same-sex couples. The question is: why now? And why New York? I believe both answers start at the Stonewall Inn. When the Village erupted in protest forty-two years ago next month, New York—and every other state in the union, save one—still had laws on the books that made same-sex relationships a crime. A couple could go to prison for years, just for being intimate in the privacy of their own home. For men and women of that era, an era many of us remember well, being in a gay relationship meant living in fear: Fear of police harassment. Fear of public humiliation. Fear of workplace discrimination. Fear of physical violence.

Today, in some places, those fears still linger. But as a nation, we have come a long way since Stonewall. Today, two women in a committed relationship—who years ago would have hidden their relationship from family and friends—will instead take part in a wedding ceremony in front of their family and friends. Today, two men who are long-time partners—who years ago would never even have entertained the idea—will adopt a child and begin a family.

Both events are possible because thousands of courageous individuals risked everything to come out and speak out. And because they did—because they organized and protested, because they poured their hearts out to friends and family and neighbors, because they stood up for their rights and marched for equality and ran for office—laws banning same-sex relationships have been struck down by the Supreme Court. More than twenty states have adopted laws that prohibit discrimination based on sexual orientation. And beginning this year, patriotic men and women will be able to enlist in the US military without having to hide their identity.

We owe all of those pioneers a deep debt of gratitude. And although the work is far from over, there is no doubt that we have passed the tipping point.

Today, a majority of Americans support marriage equality—and young people increasingly view marriage equality in much the same way as young people in the 1960s viewed civil rights. Eventually, as happened with civil rights for African Americans, they will be a majority of voters. And they will pass laws that reflect their values and elect presidents who personify them.

It is not a matter of if—but when.

And the question for every New York State lawmaker is: do you want to be remembered as a leader on civil rights or an obstructionist? Remember, on matters of freedom and equality, history has not remembered obstructionists kindly. Not on abolition. Not on women's suffrage. Not on workers' rights. Not on civil rights. And it will be no different on marriage rights.

Why now? Because this is our time to stand up for equality. This is our time to conquer the next frontier of freedom. This is our time to be as bold and brave as the pioneers who came before us. And this is our time to lead the American journey forward.

You know, it's fitting that the gay rights movement began in our city, because New Yorkers have always been at the forefront of movements to expand American freedoms—and guarantee American liberties. Long before our Founding Fathers wisely decided to separate church from state, leading citizens of our city petitioned their colonial rulers for religious freedom. Long before Lincoln signed the Emancipation Proclamation, many New Yorkers—including the founder of this college, Peter Cooper—crusaded against slavery. Long before the nation adopted the Nineteenth Amendment, New Yorkers helped lead the movement for women's suffrage. And long before the Civil Rights Act of 1964, New Yorkers played a pivotal role in advancing a color-blind society.

So why should New York lead on marriage equality right now? Because we have always led the charge for freedom—and we have always led by example. No place in the world is more committed to freedom of expression—religious, artistic, political, social, personal— than New York City. And no place in the world is more welcoming to all people, no matter what their ethnicity or orientation.

That's what always has set us apart. In our city, there is no shame in being true to yourself. There is only pride. We take you as you are—and we let you be who you wish to be. That is the essence of New York City.

That is what makes us a safe haven for people of every background and orientation . . . and a magnet for talented and creative people. It's the reason why we are the economic engine for the country and the greatest city in the world.

But it's up to us to keep it that way. As other states recognize the rights of same-sex couples to marry, we cannot stand by and watch. To do so would be to betray our civic values and history—and it would harm our competitive edge in the global economy. This is an issue of democratic principles—but make no mistake, it carries economic consequences.

We are the freest city in the freest country in the world—but freedom is not frozen in time. And if we are to remain the freest city, with the most dynamic and innovative economy, we must lead on this issue—just as we have on so many other matters of fundamental civil rights.

In talking to state legislators who do not yet support marriage equality, I can sense that many of them are searching their souls for answers—and they are torn. Like all of us, they have friends and family and colleagues who are gay and lesbian. They know gay and lesbian couples who are deeply in love with each other—many of whom are loving and devoted parents, as well. They know those couples yearn to be seen and treated as equal to all other couples. And they often hear from their own families—especially their children—that this is a civil rights issue. I hope they listen to their kids carefully and make them proud with their foresight and courage.

Now, I understand the desire of some to seek guidance from their religious teachings. But this is not a religious issue. This a civil issue. And that is why, under the bill proposed in Albany, no church or synagogue or mosque would be required to perform or sanction a same-sex wedding—as is the case in every other state that has legalized marriage equality.

Some faith communities would perform them; others would not. That is their right. I have enormous respect for religious leaders on both sides of the issue, but government has no business taking sides in these debates—none.

As private individuals, we may be part of a faith community that forbids divorce or birth control or alcohol. But as public citizens, we do not impose those prohibitions on society. We may place our personal faith in the Torah, or the New Testament, or the Koran, or anything else. But as a civil society, we place our *public* faith in the US Constitution: the principles and protections that define it, and the values that have guided its evolution. And as elected officials, our responsibility is not to any one creed or congregation, but to all citizens.

It is my hope that a majority of the State Senate will recognize that supporting marriage equality is not only consistent with our civic principles—it is consistent with *conservative* principles. Conservatives believe that government should not intrude into people's personal lives—and it's just none of the government's business who you love.

Conservatives also believe that government should not stand in the way of free markets and private associations—including contracts between consenting parties. And that's exactly what marriage is: a contract, a legal bond, between two adults who vow to support one another, in sickness and in health.

There is no state interest in denying one class of couples a right to that contract. Just the opposite, in fact. Marriage has always been a force for stability in families and communities—because it fosters responsibility. That's why conservatives promote marriage—and that's why marriage equality would be healthy for society, healthy for couples, and healthy for children.

Right now, sadly, children of some same-sex couples often ask their parents: "Why haven't you gotten married like all our friends' parents?" That's a heartbreaking question to answer.

And it's an early expression of the profound principle that sets our country apart: that all people are created equal, with equal rights to life, liberty, and the pursuit of happiness. That is the American dream—but for gay and lesbian couples, it is still only that: a dream.

The plain reality is, if we are to recognize same-sex and opposite-sex couples as equals, that equality must extend to obtaining civil marriage licenses. Now, some people ask: why not just grant gay couples civil unions?

That is a fair and honest question. But the answer is simply unavoidable: long ago, the Supreme Court declared that "separate but equal" opportunities are inherently unequal. It took the Supreme Court nearly sixty years after *Plessy v. Ferguson*, which upheld disparate treatment of non-whites, to come to that conclusion.

But justice finally prevailed. It took the Supreme Court another thirteen years to strike down laws barring interracial marriage and another thirty-six years after that to strike down laws criminalizing same-sex relationships. The march for equality and tolerance in America has sometimes been slow, but it has never stopped.

Since our nation's earliest days, when the Congress first adopted the Bill of Rights, the Constitution's protections of liberty have grown broader and stronger, and the law of the land has grown increasingly neutral on matters of race, nationality, gender, and sexual orientation.

That inexorable progress is the genius of our constitutional system. In fact, we have had major social change without violence because the revolution that we seek is contained within our founding documents. We have no king to overthrow—only our own ideals to live up to.

In the weeks ahead, I will continue doing everything I can to convince our state legislators to take the long view and consider their place in history—and consider the kind of world they want to leave their children.

Governor Cuomo and Governor Paterson both deserve great credit for advancing this issue in Albany, and I strongly believe that just as New Yorkers are discussing and debating it openly—so should both houses of the state legislature.

That's democracy. And the essence of democracy is a public debate and a public vote. New Yorkers have a right to know where their elected officials stand. We deserve a vote not next year, or after the 2012 elections, but in this legislative session.

There's a reason I'm so passionate about this issue—and so determined to push for change. I see the pain the status quo causes—and I cannot defend it. When I meet a New Yorker who is gay, when I speak with members and family members of my staff who are gay, or when I look into the eyes of my niece Rachel, I cannot tell them that their government is correct in denying them the right to marry. I cannot tell them that marriage is not for them. I cannot tell them that a civil union is good enough.

In our democracy, near-equality is no equality. Government either treats everyone the same, or it doesn't. And right now, it doesn't.

Tonight, two New Yorkers who are in a committed relationship will come home, cook dinner, help their kids with their homework, and turn in for the night. They want desperately to be married—not for the piece of paper they will get. Not for the ceremony or the reception or the wedding cake. But for the recognition that the lifelong commitment they have made to each other is not less than anyone else's and not second class in any way. And they want it not just for themselves—but for their children. They want their children to know that their family is as healthy and legitimate as all other families.

That desire for equal standing in society is extraordinarily powerful and it has led to extraordinary advances in American freedom.

It has never been defeated. It cannot be defeated. And on marriage equality, it will not be defeated.

There is no retreating to a past that has disappeared. There is no holding back a wave that has crested. And there is no denying a freedom that belongs to all of us.

The time has come for us to fulfill the dreams that exploded onto Sheridan Square forty-two years ago: to allow thousands of men and women to become full members of the American family, and to take the next step on the inspired journey our Founding Fathers first began.

Together, we can work across the aisle to pass a bill allowing all New Yorkers to walk down the aisle and lead our state and country toward a more perfect union. This is something that we have to do, and we have to do it right now. We are Americans, and this is what America stands for. Thank you very much.

GOVERNOR ANDREW CUOMO (1957–)

When Andrew Cuomo was running for governor of New York, he pledged he would push for gay marriage if elected. He won, and within six months of taking office, he signed the Marriage Equality Act into law, making New York the fifth state and sixth jurisdiction (after Washington, DC) to issue marriage licenses to same-sex couples. One month later, on July 24, 2011, the law went into effect. Six Republican senators were convinced to vote in favor of the law, knowing that it might mean the end of their political career—and in at least one case, it probably was. Senator Roy McDonald was narrowly defeated in a primary challenge by gay-marriage opponent Kathleen Marchione.

A New Level of Social Justice
Governor Andrew Cuomo
June 24, 2011

I want to thank the people of the State of New York who were engaged in this session. We reached out to them through e-mails, through all sorts of forums all across the state, the advocacy organizations reached out to them, and they weighed in, and they made a difference. Democracy works when the people speak, and the people spoke in volumes over these past few months, and this legislature responded this week to their calls. I truly believe this state is on a different trajectory than it was six months ago.

New York as a state, when it is at its finest, is a beacon for social justice. The legacy of this state was that we were the progressive capital of the nation. And when you look back at so many of the great progressive movements that were birthed here in New York—the women's rights movement was birthed here in New York, the environmental rights movement was birthed here in New York, Storm King on the Hudson, the workers' rights movement was birthed here in New York after the Triangle Shirtwaist Factory fire—all these great progressive movements—the gay rights movement was birthed at Stonewall. And what this state said today brings this discussion of marriage equality to a new plane. That's the power and the beauty of New York. The other states look to New York for the progressive direction, and what we said today is, "You look to New York once again."

Because New York made a powerful statement, not just for the people of New York but the people all across this nation. We reached a new level of social justice this evening. Marriage equality. I said to the legislators, "You look at the first word, *marriage*—it's really about the second word, *equality*." It's really about New Yorkers, our brothers and sisters, looking at us and saying, "We want equality. We want equality in society, equality in our relationships, equality in our love, equality in our families— we want full recognition. Marriage equality." And we did it today. And that legislature worked together and they responded to their better angels.

They responded to their hopes, not their fears: twenty-nine out of thirty Democrats. Four Republicans who showed real courage. Senator Alesi, who's with us here today, let's give him a round of applause. And even the way we worked together to make it happen. Senator Tom Duane and Assemblyman Dan O'Donnell who have been fighting this for years. I applaud Mayor Mike Bloomberg who stepped up to the plate and really, really worked. I applaud Governor David Paterson who put this on the radar screen and on the agenda years ago, and tried to pass it. You know, sometimes justice is an evolutionary process, and Governor Paterson and that first vote is an evolutionary process to where we are today.

I thank the advocacy community that came together from all across the nation and worked as one, and they were sophisticated and they were smart and they were constructive in their effort and it was my pleasure to work with them.

I'm always proud to be a New Yorker, but tonight I am especially proud to be a New Yorker.

And last, but not least, I want to thank the greatest team of government professionals ever assembled—all these things that we did . . . it's a pleasure.

Thank you.

SECRETARY OF STATE HILLARY CLINTON (1947–)

At the Beijing Women's Conference in 1995, Hillary Clinton inspired the world when she announced unequivocally: "Human rights are women's rights and women's rights are human rights." Until then, gender had been seen as a marginal offshoot of human rights concerns; Clinton redefined human rights to include women. More than fifteen years later, as secretary of state, Clinton once again redefined human rights in her Human Rights Day remarks to a UN audience in Switzerland. While the speech doesn't directly discuss marriage equality, she calls persuasively for full human rights for gay people. Since access to love, family, and commitment is more than a human right, it's a need—and one that makes us most human—her words poignantly convey the morality of marriage equality.

Human Rights Day Speech
Secretary of State Hillary Clinton
December 6, 2011

Good evening, and let me express my deep honor and pleasure at being here. I want to thank Director General Tokayev and Ms. Wyden, along with other ministers, ambassadors, excellencies, and UN partners.

This weekend we will celebrate Human Rights Day, the anniversary of one of the great accomplishments of the last century.

Beginning in 1947, delegates from six continents devoted themselves to drafting a declaration that would enshrine the fundamental rights and freedoms of people everywhere. In the aftermath of World War II, many nations pressed for a statement of this kind to help ensure that we would prevent future atrocities and protect the inherent humanity and dignity of all people. And so the delegates went to work. They discussed, they wrote, they revisited, revised, rewrote, for thousands of hours. And they incorporated suggestions and revisions from governments, organizations, and individuals around the world.

At three o'clock in the morning on December 10, 1948, after nearly two years of drafting and one last long night of debate, the president of the UN General Assembly called for a vote on the final text. Forty-eight nations voted in favor; eight abstained; none dissented. And the Universal Declaration of Human Rights was adopted. It proclaims a simple, powerful idea: all human beings are born free and equal in dignity and rights. And with the declaration, it was made clear that rights are not conferred by government; they are the birthright of all people. It does not matter what country we live in, who our leaders are, or even who we are. Because we are human, we therefore have rights. And because we have rights, governments are bound to protect them.

In the sixty-three years since the declaration was adopted, many nations have made great progress in making human rights a human reality. Step by step, barriers that once prevented people from enjoying the full measure of liberty, the full experience of dignity, and the full benefits of humanity have fallen away. In many places, racist laws have been repealed, legal and social practices that relegated women to second-class status have been abolished, the ability of religious minorities to practice their faith freely has been secured.

In most cases, this progress was not easily won. People fought and organized and campaigned in public squares and private spaces to change not only laws, but hearts and minds. And thanks to that work of generations, millions of individuals whose lives were once narrowed by injustice are now able to live more freely and to participate more fully in the political, economic, and social lives of their communities.

Now, there is still, as you all know, much more to be done to secure that commitment, that reality, and progress for all people. Today, I want to talk about the work we have left to do to protect one group of people whose human rights are still denied in too many parts of the world today. In many ways, they are an invisible minority. They are arrested, beaten, terrorized, even executed. Many are treated with contempt and violence by their fellow citizens while authorities empowered to protect them look the other way or, too often, even join in the abuse. They are denied opportunities to work and learn, driven from their homes and countries, and forced to suppress or deny who they are to protect themselves from harm.

I am talking about gay, lesbian, bisexual, and transgender people, human beings born free and bestowed equality and dignity, who have a right to claim that,

which is now one of the remaining human rights challenges of our time. I speak about this subject knowing
that my own country's record on human rights for gay
people is far from perfect. Until 2003, it was still a crime
in parts of our country. Many LGBT Americans have endured violence and harassment in their own lives, and
for some, including many young people, bullying and
exclusion are daily experiences. So we, like all nations,
have more work to do to protect human rights at home.

Now, raising this issue, I know, is sensitive for many
people and the obstacles standing in the way of protecting the human rights of LGBT people rest on deeply
held personal, political, cultural, and religious beliefs.
So I come here before you with respect, understanding,
and humility. Even though progress on this front is not
easy, we cannot delay acting. So in that spirit, I want to
talk about the difficult and important issues we must
address together to reach a global consensus that recognizes the human rights of LGBT citizens everywhere.

The first issue goes to the heart of the matter. Some
have suggested that gay rights and human rights are
separate and distinct; but, in fact, they are one and the
same. Now, of course, sixty years ago, the governments
that drafted and passed the Universal Declaration of Human Rights were not thinking about how it applied to
the LGBT community. They also weren't thinking about
how it applied to indigenous people or children or people with disabilities or other marginalized groups. Yet
in the past sixty years, we have come to recognize that
members of these groups are entitled to the full measure
of dignity and rights, because, like all people, they share
a common humanity.

This recognition did not occur all at once. It evolved over time. And as it did, we understood that we were honoring rights that people always had, rather than creating new or special rights for them. Like being a woman, like being a racial, religious, tribal, or ethnic minority, being LGBT does not make you less human. And that is why gay rights are human rights, and human rights are gay rights.

It is a violation of human rights when people are beaten or killed because of their sexual orientation, or because they do not conform to cultural norms about how men and women should look or behave. It is a violation of human rights when governments declare it illegal to be gay, or allow those who harm gay people to go unpunished. It is a violation of human rights when lesbian or transgendered women are subjected to so-called corrective rape, or forcibly subjected to hormone treatments, or when people are murdered after public calls for violence toward gays, or when they are forced to flee their nations and seek asylum in other lands to save their lives. And it is a violation of human rights when life-saving care is withheld from people because they are gay, or equal access to justice is denied to people because they are gay, or public spaces are out of bounds to people because they are gay. No matter what we look like, where we come from, or who we are, we are all equally entitled to our human rights and dignity.

The second issue is a question of whether homosexuality arises from a particular part of the world. Some seem to believe it is a Western phenomenon, and therefore people outside the West have grounds to reject it. Well, in reality, gay people are born into and belong to every society in the world. They are all ages, all races, all faiths; they are doctors and teachers, farmers and bankers, soldiers and athletes; and whether we know it, or whether we acknowledge it, they are our family, our friends, and our neighbors.

Being gay is not a Western invention; it is a human reality. And protecting the human rights of all people, gay or straight, is not something that only Western governments do. South Africa's constitution, written in the aftermath of apartheid, protects the equality of all citizens, including gay people. In Colombia and Argentina, the rights of gays are also legally protected. In Nepal, the supreme court has ruled that equal rights apply to LGBT citizens. The government of Mongolia has committed to pursue new legislation that will tackle antigay discrimination.

Now, some worry that protecting the human rights of the LGBT community is a luxury that only wealthy nations can afford. But, in fact, in all countries there are costs to not protecting these rights—in both gay and straight lives lost to disease and violence, and the silencing of voices and views that would strengthen communities, in ideas never pursued by entrepreneurs who happen to be gay. Costs are incurred whenever any group is treated as lesser or the other, whether they are women, racial or religious minorities, or the LGBT. Former President Mogae of Botswana pointed out recently that for as long as LGBT people are kept in the shadows, there cannot be an effective public health program to tackle HIV and AIDS. Well, that holds true for other challenges as well.

The third, and perhaps most challenging, issue arises

when people cite religious or cultural values as a reason to violate or not to protect the human rights of LGBT citizens. This is not unlike the justification offered for violent practices toward women like honor killings, widow burning, or female genital mutilation. Some people still defend those practices as part of a cultural tradition. But violence toward women isn't cultural; it's criminal. Likewise with slavery: what was once justified as sanctioned by God is now properly reviled as an unconscionable violation of human rights.

In each of these cases, we came to learn that no practice or tradition trumps the human rights that belong to all of us. And this holds true for inflicting violence on LGBT people, criminalizing their status or behavior, expelling them from their families and communities, or tacitly or explicitly accepting their killing.

Of course, it bears noting that rarely are cultural and religious traditions and teachings actually in conflict with the protection of human rights. Indeed, our religion and our culture are sources of compassion and inspiration toward our fellow human beings. It was not only those who've justified slavery who leaned on religion, it was also those who sought to abolish it. And let us keep in mind that our commitments to protect the freedom of religion and to defend the dignity of LGBT people emanate from a common source. For many of us, religious belief and practice is a vital source of meaning and identity, and fundamental to who we are as people. And likewise, for most of us, the bonds of love and family that we forge are also vital sources of meaning and identity. And caring for others is an expression of what it means to be fully human. It is because the human experience is universal that human rights are universal and cut across all religions and cultures.

The fourth issue is what history teaches us about how we make progress toward rights for all. Progress starts with honest discussion. Now, there are some who say and believe that all gay people are pedophiles, that homosexuality is a disease that can be caught or cured, or that gays recruit others to become gay. Well, these notions are simply not true. They are also unlikely to disappear if those who promote or accept them are dismissed out of hand rather than invited to share their fears and concerns. No one has ever abandoned a belief because he was forced to do so.

Universal human rights include freedom of expression and freedom of belief, even if our words or beliefs denigrate the humanity of others. Yet, while we are each free to believe whatever we choose, we cannot *do* whatever we choose, not in a world where we protect the human rights of all.

Reaching understanding of these issues takes more than speech. It does take a conversation. In fact, it takes a constellation of conversations in places big and small. And it takes a willingness to see stark differences in belief as a reason to begin the conversation, not to avoid it.

But progress comes from changes in laws. In many places, including my own country, legal protections have preceded, not followed, broader recognition of rights. Laws have a teaching effect. Laws that discriminate validate other kinds of discrimination. Laws that require equal protections reinforce the moral imperative of equality. And practically speaking, it is often the case that laws must change before fears about change dissipate.

Many in my country thought that President Truman was making a grave error when he ordered the racial desegregation of our military. They argued that it would undermine unit cohesion. And it wasn't until he went ahead and did it that we saw how it strengthened our social fabric in ways even the supporters of the policy could not foresee. Likewise, some worried in my country that the repeal of "Don't Ask, Don't Tell" would have a negative effect on our armed forces. Now, the Marine Corps commandant, who was one of the strongest voices against the repeal, says that his concerns were unfounded and that the Marines have embraced the change.

Finally, progress comes from being willing to walk a mile in someone else's shoes. We need to ask ourselves, *How would it feel if it were a crime to love the person I love? How would it feel to be discriminated against for something about myself that I cannot change?* This challenge applies to all of us as we reflect upon deeply held beliefs, as we work to embrace tolerance and respect for the dignity of all persons, and as we engage humbly with those with whom we disagree in the hope of creating greater understanding.

A fifth and final question is how we do our part to bring the world to embrace human rights for all people including LGBT people. Yes, LGBT people must help lead this effort, as so many of you are. Their knowledge and experiences are invaluable and their courage inspirational. We know the names of brave LGBT activists who have literally given their lives for this cause, and there are many more whose names we will never know. But often those who are denied rights are least empowered to bring about the changes they seek. Acting alone, minorities can never achieve the majorities necessary for political change.

So when any part of humanity is sidelined, the rest of us cannot sit on the sidelines. Every time a barrier to progress has fallen, it has taken a cooperative effort from those on both sides of the barrier. In the fight for women's rights, the support of men remains crucial. The fight for racial equality has relied on contributions from people of all races. Combating Islamophobia or anti-Semitism is a task for people of all faiths. And the same is true with this struggle for equality.

Conversely, when we see denials and abuses of human rights and fail to act, that sends the message to those deniers and abusers that they won't suffer any consequences for their actions, and so they carry on. But when we do act, we send a powerful moral message. Right here in Geneva, the international community acted this year to strengthen a global consensus around the human rights of LGBT people. At the Human Rights Council in March, eighty-five countries from all regions supported a statement calling for an end to criminalization and violence against people because of their sexual orientation and gender identity.

At the following session of the council in June, South Africa took the lead on a resolution about violence against LGBT people. The delegation from South Africa spoke eloquently about their own experience and struggle for human equality and its indivisibility. When the measure passed, it became the first-ever UN resolution recognizing the human rights of gay people worldwide. In the Organization of American States this year, the

Inter-American Commission on Human Rights created a unit on the rights of LGBT people, a step toward what we hope will be the creation of a special rapporteur.

Now, we must go further and work here and in every region of the world to galvanize more support for the human rights of the LGBT community. To the leaders of those countries where people are jailed, beaten, or executed for being gay, I ask you to consider this: leadership, by definition, means being out in front of your people when it is called for. It means standing up for the dignity of all your citizens and persuading your people to do the same. It also means ensuring that all citizens are treated as equals under your laws, because let me be clear—I am not saying that gay people can't or don't commit crimes. They can and they do, just like straight people. And when they do, they should be held accountable, but it should never be a crime to be gay.

And to people of all nations, I say supporting human rights is your responsibility too. The lives of gay people are shaped not only by laws, but by the treatment they receive every day from their families, from their neighbors. Eleanor Roosevelt, who did so much to advance human rights worldwide, said that these rights begin in the small places close to home—the streets where people live, the schools they attend, the factories, farms, and offices where they work. These places are your domain. The actions you take, the ideals that you advocate, can determine whether human rights flourish where you are.

And finally, to LGBT men and women worldwide, let me say this: wherever you live and whatever the circumstances of your life, whether you are connected to a network of support or feel isolated and vulnerable, please know that you are not alone. People around the globe are working hard to support you and to bring an end to the injustices and dangers you face. That is certainly true for my country. And you have an ally in the United States of America and you have millions of friends among the American people.

The Obama administration defends the human rights of LGBT people as part of our comprehensive human rights policy and as a priority of our foreign policy. In our embassies, our diplomats are raising concerns about specific cases and laws, and working with a range of partners to strengthen human rights protections for all. In Washington, we have created a task force at the State Department to support and coordinate this work. And in the coming months, we will provide every embassy with a toolkit to help improve their efforts. And we have created a program that offers emergency support to defenders of human rights for LGBT people.

This morning, back in Washington, President Obama put into place the first US government strategy dedicated to combating human rights abuses against LGBT persons abroad. Building on efforts already underway at the State Department and across the government, the president has directed all US government agencies engaged overseas to combat the criminalization of LGBT status and conduct, to enhance efforts to protect vulnerable LGBT refugees and asylum seekers, to ensure that our foreign assistance promotes the protection of LGBT rights, to enlist international organizations in the fight against discrimination, and to respond swiftly to abuses against LGBT persons.

I am also pleased to announce that we are launching a new Global Equality Fund that will support the work of civil society organizations working on these issues around the world. This fund will help them record facts so they can target their advocacy, learn how to use the law as a tool, manage their budgets, train their staffs, and forge partnerships with women's organizations and other human rights groups. We have committed more than three million dollars to start this fund, and we have hope that others will join us in supporting it.

The women and men who advocate for human rights for the LGBT community in hostile places, some of whom are here today with us, are brave and dedicated, and deserve all the help we can give them. We know the road ahead will not be easy. A great deal of work lies before us. But many of us have seen firsthand how quickly change can come. In our lifetimes, attitudes toward gay people in many places have been transformed. Many people, including myself, have experienced a deepening of our own convictions on this topic over the years, as we have devoted more thought to it, engaged in dialogues and debates, and established personal and professional relationships with people who are gay.

This evolution is evident in many places. To highlight one example, the Delhi high court decriminalized homosexuality in India two years ago, writing, and I quote, "If there is one tenet that can be said to be an underlying theme of the Indian constitution, it is inclusiveness." There is little doubt in my mind that support for LGBT human rights will continue to climb. Because for many young people, this is simple: all people deserve to be treated with dignity and have their human rights respected, no matter who they are or whom they love.

There is a phrase that people in the United States invoke when urging others to support human rights: *Be on the right side of history.* The story of the United States is the story of a nation that has repeatedly grappled with intolerance and inequality. We fought a brutal civil war over slavery. People from coast to coast joined in campaigns to recognize the rights of women, indigenous peoples, racial minorities, children, people with disabilities, immigrants, workers, and on and on. And the march toward equality and justice has continued. Those who advocate for expanding the circle of human rights were and are on the right side of history, and history honors them. Those who tried to constrict human rights were wrong, and history reflects that as well.

I know that the thoughts I've shared today involve questions on which opinions are still evolving. As it has happened so many times before, opinion will converge once again with the truth, the immutable truth, that all persons are created free and equal in dignity and rights. We are called once more to make real the words of the Universal Declaration. Let us answer that call. Let us be on the right side of history, for our people, our nations, and future generations, whose lives will be shaped by the work we do today. I come before you with great hope and confidence that no matter how long the road ahead, we will travel it successfully together. Thank you very much.

MAYOR CORY BOOKER (1969–)

As the young, progressive mayor of Newark, New Jersey, Cory Booker has proven to be ahead of the curve on many issues. As an African American leader, he is (along with President Obama, Representative John Lewis, athletes such as Jason Collins and Wade Davis, and others) certainly chipping away at homophobia that can be part of socially conservative values among some African Americans.

When Chris Christie, the governor of New Jersey, vetoed a 2012 bill legalizing gay marriage in New Jersey, Mayor Booker used a general press conference, excerpted here, to spontaneously elucidate his passionate feelings about the issue.

To Me This Is Infuriating
Mayor Cory Booker
January 26, 2012

I've got very, very strong feelings about this . . . but dear God, we should not be putting civil rights issues to a popular vote subject to the sentiments and the passions of the day. No minority should have their rights subject to the passions and sentiments of the majority. This is the fundamental bedrock of what our nation stands for.

I get very concerned that we have created a second-class citizenship in our state. That's what we have in America right now. We have two classes of citizens. Jackie Robinson said that the right of every American to first-class citizenship is the most important issue of our time. Let's stop the ruse. We have two types of citizens right now in our state: citizens like me, who, if I choose to marry somebody, I can marry somebody.

[I can marry someone] from a different country and they have a right to a United States citizenship. I talked to somebody last night, his spouse is looking to be deported. His *spouse* is looking to be deported. If I'm [married and I] die, this first-class citizenship that I have says that my wife will get to avoid my estate taxes. The second-class citizens in this country don't have those rights. There's over a thousand federal laws that create different classes of American citizenship because we're not treating everybody equally under the law. I read the Fourteenth Amendment clearly. It talks about "equal protection of the laws." And that was never something that should go up to a popular vote, whether blacks, women, or other minorities, [all] should be equal first-class citizens. Thank God there wasn't a popular vote whether Jackie Robinson should become a professional baseball player.

To me this is infuriating that we are in the twenty-first century and we haven't created equality under the law. And so I will be—fundamentally in the fiber of my being—supportive of equal citizenship for all people in this country, because I know that at the end of the day, I would not be here, my family wouldn't be able to put food on the table for me, if it wasn't for that ideal in America.

Don't just point to [Governor Christie]. We had the chance to do this under the last governor, and we didn't have the courage to stand up and do the right thing. So I'm tired and exhausted that we have a country that has been able to overcome women having a second-class position in this country, blacks having a second-class position in this country, Latinos having a second-class citizenship in this country, blacks and whites who want to marry having a second-class citizenship in this country [but not overcome second-class citizenship for gay people]. It's about time we create first-class citizenship for every American, plain and simple. Every New Jerseyan. This should not be a popular vote. This is something we should do now . . . To me, it's ridiculous and offensive that we're still having this debate in Trenton. It should have been done months, if not years, ago.

PRESIDENT BILL CLINTON (1946–)

President Clinton's middle-of-the-night signing of the Defense of Marriage Act in 1996 did permanent damage to his relationship with gay activists and supporters, who had believed his commitment to their right to live openly and with dignity. At the 2013 GLAAD Awards, where he accepted an award for his support of LGBT rights, he spoke out against DOMA. "You signed it!" an angry audience member called out, an act during his presidency for which Clinton has been reluctant to take responsibility.

On March 7, 2013, a month before the GLAAD awards, President Clinton wrote a *Washington Post* op-ed entitled "It's Time to Overturn DOMA," attempting to explain—and correct—his earlier action. He begins with the obvious:

> In 1996, I signed the Defense of Marriage Act. Although that was only seventeen years ago, it was a very different time. In no state in the union was same-sex marriage recognized, much less available as a legal right, but some were moving in that direction. Washington, as a result, was swirling with all manner of possible responses, some quite draconian.

President Clinton then describes that, behind the scenes, a bipartisan group of former senators filed an amicus brief with the Supreme Court stating that they

believed the passage of DOMA "would defuse a movement to enact a constitutional amendment banning gay
marriage, which would have ended the debate for a generation or more." When DOMA came to his desk, it was
overwhelmingly supported by Congress—and opposed
by a mere 81 of the 535 members. Given that support, as
well as his hope that federally defining marriage as between a man and a woman was a safer route than risking
a constitutional amendment banning gay marriage, he
signed the bill.

But President Clinton goes beyond attempting to
justify the hard place in which he found himself when
he signed DOMA into law; he admits fault.

> On March 27, DOMA will come before the Supreme Court,
> and the justices must decide whether it is consistent with
> the principles of a nation that honors freedom, equality
> and justice above all, and is therefore constitutional. As the
> president who signed the act into law, I have come to believe
> that DOMA is contrary to those principles and, in fact, in-
> compatible with our Constitution . . .
>
> When I signed the bill, I included a statement with the
> admonition that "enactment of this legislation should not,
> despite the fierce and at times divisive rhetoric surrounding
> it, be understood to provide an excuse for discrimination."
> Reading those words today, I know now that, even worse
> than providing an excuse for discrimination, the law is itself
> discriminatory.

Listing the now-familiar litany of bigotries that were
once just called life (slavery, lack of suffrage), Clinton
writes:

While our laws may at times lag behind our best natures, in the end they catch up to our core values. One hundred fifty years ago, in the midst of the Civil War, President Abraham Lincoln concluded a message to Congress by posing the very question we face today: it is not "Can any of us imagine better?" but "Can we all do better?" The answer is of course and always yes.

AFTERWORD
A SLOW GATHERING OF COURAGE
GOVERNOR MADELEINE M. KUNIN

As Woody Allen said, 80 percent of success is showing up. As a former politician I would raise that figure even higher. When I was governor of Vermont, almost everywhere I made an appearance, my presence made a statement. Showing up at an event was like a public seal of approval. I entered the room and people stopped talking; the klieg lights turned on.

Getting there was easy. (I was driven by a state trooper.) Deciding *whether* to get there was complicated. Every stop on my almost 24/7 calendar had a purpose. Who would I please by gracing their dinner, lunch, or breakfast with my presence? Who might I offend by not showing up? Some invitations to events were command performances. The governor had always shown up at the annual meeting of the state chamber of commerce, or the AFL-CIO convention every year since anyone could remember; whether it was an election year or not, Republicans and Democrats alike. My absence would be noticed.

And then there were conflicting events. I had already said yes to the teachers convention, weeks ago, and now the Burlington Rotary Club wanted me to speak on the same date at the same time. A juggling routine began as my staff and I figured out how I could get to two places at once, defying the limits of geography.

The biggest pile of invitations (before e-mail) came from sponsors of events that were discretionary. Yes or no? Those took the most time to decide. How many people would be there, would there be press, who would I please, and who might I offend? Yes, politics did raise its head. Would I gain popularity or lose it?

When I received the invitation one day in June of 1986 to speak at the gay pride parade down Church Street in Burlington, Vermont, I paused. So did my staff. I don't recall precisely what went through my mind at that moment, but while I could easily have said no (as most politicians did), I knew I had to say yes.

By saying yes, I was making a statement of support for the gay and lesbian community. I had taken a small step in that direction soon after I was elected—I had appointed an official liaison with the gay community. That was a first, both for them and for me. But it was between us. Having a liaison meeting with me at the office was not like showing up in public and hearing the cameras click.

When my trooper stopped the car close to the steps that lead to the doors of the white-steepled Unitarian church at the head of Church Street, I was nervous. One glance at the boisterous crowd and I knew this would not be like any majorette-led parade that I had ever attended. During the 1980s, the gay and lesbian community enjoyed being outrageous. The scourge of AIDS hadn't yet descended. This event was a wild and colorful celebration. The statement the gay marchers made was not yet a clear demand for equal rights; it was a demand for recognition: *We are here. See us, hear us, and listen to us.*

Showing up at the parade was more of a test of courage for the marchers than for me. It marked the first coming out for many men and women. That excitement of liberation from the confines of the closet combined with the thrill of mutual recognition (*You too?*) exploded into joy. I was pulled into the drum-beating, feet-stomping crowd and no longer wanted to hold myself apart. The exuberance of the moment embraced me.

I do not remember what I said that morning. I wish I did. It must have been supportive, because I recall the cheers, but it's possible they didn't cheer me for what I said—those in the back could not have heard me—but for the simple fact that I was there with them.

As governor, I knew about contrasts, going from one event to another, tasting different slices of life, from birthday celebrations to funerals. But no contrast was more clear than going from the gay pride parade in Burlington in the morning to the Veterans of Foreign Wars celebration twenty-two miles north in St. Albans that afternoon. "Up the road a piece," as a Vermonter might say. I found myself marching in step with the standard-bearing, uniformed, medal-bedecked veterans, flags held high, as we paraded on the quiet tree-lined town green. The only sounds heard were the ritual shouts of commands, promptly obeyed, as they had long practiced.

What if they knew where I just was? I thought to myself, the rainbow-colored scene I had just left still bouncing in my mind's eye. *What would they think?* Could I even have felt disloyal to the veterans for having been there?

Impossible to believe that now, but then, in the late 1980s, these were two different worlds. They marched in different steps, and thought in different ways. The gay pride crowd sought to break tradition; the veterans were there to maintain it.

What then could be seen as an act of courage on my part would not cause one eyebrow to be raised today. The unexpected became the expected. Neither group of marchers could have dreamed that some thirty years later, gay soldiers would openly serve in the military and same-sex marriage would be legal in Vermont and twelve other states (plus the District of Columbia)— including California, as a result of the June 2013 Supreme Court decision on Proposition 8. Today, 30 percent of Americans live in states that permit same-sex marriage. These citizens are now eligible for federal benefits, thanks to the court's 5–4 decision to strike down the Defense of Marriage Act. This marked a dramatic turning point in the forty-year struggle for equal rights. As one of the plaintiffs in the California case said, "Now I can tell my children that we are a family, just like everybody else."

Just like everybody else—that is the essence of equality.

But not everyone can benefit from these historic decisions. Those who live in the thirty-seven states that still ban same-sex marriage remain on the waiting list. Indeed, in many parts of the country and amongst some religious groups, gay marriage remains taboo, evidenced by the thirty-one states that passed constitutional amendments to ban gay and lesbian unions. (The two Supreme Court decisions in June 2013 didn't render all of those bans unconstitutional, but as new states continue to sign on to legalizing same-sex marriage, it's likely that they will soon become a shameful relic of the past.) The campaign for same-sex marriage, regarded as radical at the outset, today is seen by many as just the opposite—a reach for tradition. Marriage, for any couple, straight or gay, imposes structure on the relationship and affords the imprimatur of belonging. The turning point came in 2004 when Massachusetts became the first state to legalize same-sex marriage. No longer was the conversation only about "rights." It became about love.

Democracies have engaged in a long-standing debate about how cultural change occurs. Which comes first, law or public opinion? Fifty-one percent of Americans in a June 2013 *New York Times*/CBS News poll said yes to: "Should it be legal for same-sex couples to marry, or not?" A Pew poll taken nine years earlier, in 2004, found that 61 percent opposed same-sex marriage. That change would not have been possible without the political power of the gay community, the growing understanding of the straight community, and the power of law.

We were not there yet in 1986 when I attended my first pride event. A few days after my speech at the Unitarian church, I received a hint that my appearance at the gay pride parade did not receive uniform approval. I was told that my picture, as it appeared in the local *Burlington Free Press*, had been taped to a cash register in a general store in "the northeast kingdom," a sparsely populated region of the state. The photographer had taken pains to make sure that the banner that read *Gay Pride Day* was clearly legible. I was shown standing at the podium, underneath the banner. Someone had taken the trouble to draw a thick red circle around the photo, with a diagonal slash across it. "No."

Much of Vermont was far from ready to abandon bias and accept equality. The most ugly display of antigay bigotry occurred in Burlington when a young man, who had just left a gay bar, was found bloodied and beaten unconscious in an adjoining alleyway. For a week, it was not known whether he would live or die. The attack occurred while a legislative committee was debating whether to include gay and lesbian assaults in a hate crimes bill. It would create tougher penalties for crimes committed on the basis of racial or religious bigotry.

I decided to testify before the committee. Until that day, I had carefully observed the separation of powers that every schoolchild learns—executive, legislative, and judicial. As the executive, I had never appeared before a legislative committee. Not my territory. What made me step into it this time?

Something flashed in my mind; it was like a danger signal. I could not ignore it. I was compelled to show up. I had to make a statement that violence based on homosexuality must be strongly condemned and punished. The committee members listened to my testimony. Weeks later, as part of a large chorus of like-minded voices, our outrage was transformed into law.

As I look back, I believe I acted on instinct. My mind suddenly reeled back to Nazi Germany in the 1930s when gay men were among the first to be transported to the death camps. Instead of being forced to wear the yellow Jewish star, gay people were identified by pink triangles. My reaction was best expressed by the words of the Protestant pastor Martin Niemöller who himself spent seven years in concentration camps for opposing Hitler.

> First they came for the Socialists, and I did not speak out—
> because I was not a Socialist.
> Then they came for the trade unionists, and I did not speak
> out—because I was not a trade unionist.

Then they came for the Jews, and I did not speak out—because I was not a Jew.
Then they came for me—and there was no one left to speak for me.

I left Switzerland as a child in June 1940 at the outbreak of World War II, with my mother and brother. Because Switzerland had become surrounded by Nazi-occupied countries, I grew up under the shadow of the Holocaust. My family, both on my mother's French side and my father's German side, had been scattered by the war to England, Israel, and the United States. Not everyone was as lucky as we were. An aunt and uncle died at Theresienstadt. A cousin died in Auschwitz; his wife and daughter were hidden in Holland and survived. Others in France did not.

Tenuous as it may seem to some, I made a connection between the fate of the Jews in Europe and the young gay man lying in the Burlington alley. I felt the need to testify on the hate crimes bill and to support the gay pride marchers on Church Street because, by standing with them, they would not be alone.

I may have experienced a touch of hubris in thinking that my presence could help protect them from the alienation, ridicule, and abuse they might experience by coming out, by being exposed for the world to see, including their parents, their employers, and anyone else who might want to scrawl a red circle with a slash through it around their heads. It took more than twenty-five years for the words "I'm gay" to be safely said in growing parts of America and some other countries. And it took many years for more politicians to join the parade.

That said, a half-dozen or so Vermont legislators were in the vanguard. On March 27, 2000, when the final roll call was taken on the nation's first civil union bill, these legislators voted "Yea," knowing that their vote might spell defeat for them in the next election. Signs sprung up on Vermont roadsides: *Take Back Vermont.* No one knew its precise meaning, but the thrust was clear—repeal civil unions. Representative Bob Kinsey from Craftsbury, a dairy farmer and former Republican House leader, suffered the consequences. He was defeated twice after his vote. A majority of his constituents never forgave him, but his conscience was clear.

As I look back, I understand that I had to show up at these events, not because I was courageous, but because I was afraid. I was afraid that if I did not speak out, the disease of bigotry would go viral, spreading uncontrolled, as it did during the years of the Holocaust. Unlike my relatives who were killed simply because they were Jewish, I was a different person living in a different time and place. I was an American Jew with the power of the governor's bully pulpit to support me. It was safe for me to use my voice, to have my picture in the paper under the parade banner. On some not-yet-fully-understood level, I felt that speaking out against hatred when I had the opportunity to do so was my memorial to them—those who'd died.

There is another, more easily explained reason that I chose to show up to endorse the gay and lesbian rights movement. My daughter.

When Julia first told me that she loved a woman, I was taken aback. It was the late 1970s. I was in denial. Like many parents at that time, I thought it was a stage she would go through, and then grow out of, find a boyfriend, get married, and have kids. That's how I imagined the adult life of my daughter. Now the pieces of the picture were scattered and no longer fit together. She had become a different person than the one I had imagined. Plus, I feared for her.

I was afraid she would be vulnerable to attack, both physically and emotionally. *Life is hard enough as a woman*, I thought. *Why did she place this added burden on herself?*

Looking back, I recognize that at the time, I still thought she had a choice. It took me longer to recognize that as a lesbian, this is part of who she *is*. "It just happened, I never censored or buried it," she told me recently. Instead of harboring any thoughts of trying to change her, over the years she has changed *me*. She enabled me to not only accept her sexuality, but to go beyond acceptance to embracing who she is, with pride.

Still, on some level the mama bear part of me wanted to do what I could to protect her. That's why I had to show up, to speak up, to make her lesbianism not a dangerous aberration, but a safe and ordinary existence.

Many public figures have become advocates for LGBT rights because of their daughters and sons, their coworkers, neighbors, and friends who are gay. The greatest transformation that has taken place in this movement is that the gay community is no longer isolated as being "the other." "Those people" have names and faces and lives. "They" are "Us."

When State Representative William Lippert spoke on the floor of the Vermont House of Representatives in 2000, he moved the hearts and minds of his colleagues because they *knew him*. He was not just "queer," he was one of them. He had earned their respect as a knowledgeable and hard-working legislator. His was the face that represented a gay man.

He had had the courage to come out long before the issue of civil unions had hit the House floor. It was individuals like him who made equal rights for the gay community personal. It would not have been possible for lawmakers to vote the way they did if the gay community itself had not had the courage to come out and celebrate their own sexuality and equality.

In April 2013, Jason Collins announced: "I'm a thirty-four-year-old NBA center. I'm black. And I'm gay." He became the first openly gay player in a major male team sport. This milestone would not have been reached if the men and women who marched in the early gay pride parades had not declared themselves first.

The president of the United States could not have announced his support for same-sex marriage if people like Representative William Lippert had not told his story.

And members of an institution as traditional as the British House of Lords could not have heard Baroness Barker say, "Many years ago, I had the great fortune to meet someone. She and I have loved each other ever since." Yes, bigotry still surfaces in ugly shapes. In 2013 in the country of Georgia, clergy incited demonstrators to attack a fledgling gay pride parade. In large parts of sub-Saharan Africa, prison or even the death penalty may be the consequence of being openly gay. There are still reports of bullying, beatings, and murder even in America. And there are many Americans who, for personal or religious reasons (but not necessarily reasons of hatred), withhold their approval of homosexuality

Progress is not necessarily linear. We move forward in giant leaps, often propelled by young people, and then are forced to pull back in baby steps. But the trajectory is moving beyond tolerance, toward understanding. The gay community made the first move by stepping out into the sunlight. Politicians like myself then slowly gathered our courage to show up and join them.

We are not yet finished.

September 2013

MARRIAGE EQUALITY TIME LINE

December 31, 1966. A New Year's Eve police raid on the Black Cat Tavern, a gay bar in Los Angeles' Silverlake neighborhood, spawns days of protests and riots by a gay community unwilling to take discrimination and gay-bashing lying down.

June 12, 1967. *Loving v. Virginia* declares the Racial Integrity Act of 1924 unconstitutional and ends marriage bans based on race.

June 28, 1969. The Stonewall riots mark the first instance in American history where gays and lesbians fought back against a government-sponsored system that persecuted homosexuals. The media covers the protests, galvanizing the movement.

1973. The American Psychiatric Association announces removal of homosexuality from the *Diagnostic and Statistical Manual of Mental Disorders* and begins to promote antidiscrimination laws to protect LGBT Americans.

January 8, 1978. Harvey Milk is the first openly gay man to be elected to public office when he joins the San Francisco Board of Supervisors. He begins by delivering his "Hope" Speech, inspiring an emboldened gay community.

1982. The *Village Voice* becomes the first business to offer domestic partnership benefits, followed by the city of Berkeley in 1984.

July 14, 1983. Gerry Studds (D-MA) becomes the first

openly gay member of Congress when the House
Ethics Committee recommends he be reprimanded
for a sexual relationship with a male page. Congressman Studds is reelected to the House six more times
after coming out.

1983. "Same-Sex Marriage and Morality: The Human
Rights Vision of the Constitution," a thesis by a student named Evan Wolfson, is completed. The 140-
page manifesto becomes a blueprint for building
marriage equality.

June 30, 1986. In *Bowers v. Hardwick*, the Supreme Court
rules that homosexual sex is not protected under the
right to privacy.

May 30, 1987. Barney Frank becomes the second openly
gay member of Congress and the first sitting member
to voluntarily come out of the closet.

1992. David Mixner, a gay rights activist and political
strategist, serves as an advisor to Bill Clinton in the
1992 presidential campaign. As a "liaison to the gay
community," he organizes the first gay fundraiser for
a White House candidate.

January 1993. Award-winning singer/songwriter Me-
lissa Etheridge comes out publicly at the Triangle
Ball, the first inaugural ball held in honor of gays
and lesbians.

May 5, 1993. The gay marriage debate "begins" in Hawaii
with *Baehr v. Lewin*, which states that Hawaii cannot
keep same-sex couples from marrying without vio-
lating equal protection statutes.

December 21, 1993. "Don't Ask, Don't Tell" becomes official US policy for gay men and women serving in
the military.

May 20, 1996. *Romer v. Evans* extends to gays and lesbians the guarantees of the equal protection clause.

September 21, 1996. The Defense of Marriage Act passes and is signed by President Clinton.

April 30, 1997. Television host Ellen DeGeneres comes out on *The Oprah Winfrey Show*.

October 1, 1997. Former National Gay and Lesbian Task Force executive director Virginia Apuzzo becomes the highest-ranking openly gay official in the federal government when she is appointed assistant to the president for management and administration.

July 1, 2000. Vermont enacts civil unions, the precursor to same-sex marriage.

November 2002. David Cicilline of Providence, Rhode Island, is elected the first gay mayor of a US state capital.

June 26, 2003. *Lawrence v. Texas* strikes down sodomy laws in Texas, making same-sex activity legal in every US state and territory, effectively overturning *Bowers v. Hardwick*.

February 2004. Fourteen days into his term, San Francisco Mayor Gavin Newsom announced he will begin issuing marriage licenses to same-sex couples.

May 17, 2004. Same-sex marriage is legalized in Massachusetts.

May 14, 2005. Massachusetts Democrats endorse gay marriage in their platform, becoming the first statewide party to do so.

November 2008. Proposition 8, a state constitutional amendment, is passed in California, making it the only state that accepted and then revoked the right to same-sex marriage. The amendment ruled: "Only

194 🌀 We Do!

marriage between a man and a woman is valid or recognized in the State of California." Activists across the country are shocked out of complacency, galvanizing the movement for marriage.

April 3, 2009. Same-sex marriage is legalized in Iowa with the help of lawyer Camilla Taylor, currently director of Lambda Legal's Marriage Project.

August 12, 2009. President Obama presents Harvey Milk's nephew, Stuart Milk, with a posthumous Presidential Medal of Freedom, remarking, "His name was Harvey Milk and he was here to recruit us, all of us, to join a movement and change a nation. For much of his early life he had silenced himself. In the prime of his life he was silenced by the act of another. But in the brief time in which he spoke and ran and led, his voice stirred the aspirations of millions of people. He could become, after several attempts, one of the first openly gay Americans elected to public office. And his message of hope, hope unashamed, hope unafraid, could not ever be silenced. It was Harvey Milk who said it best: *You gotta give 'em hope.*" Lesbian tennis star Billie Jean King is awarded the Medal of Freedom at the same time.

September 25, 2009. Bill Clinton says in an interview with Anderson Cooper, "I am no longer opposed to [gay marriage]. I think if people want to make commitments that last a lifetime, they ought to be able to do it."

October 11, 2009. Governor Arnold Schwarznegger designates May 22 "Harvey Milk Day," weeks after inducting Milk into the California Hall of Fame, marking the first time any state has officially honored a gay person.

February 23, 2011. President Obama instructs the US Department of Justice to stop defending the constitutionality of DOMA. Congress is left to mount the legal defense of this federal law.

July 24, 2011. Governor Andrew Cuomo helps to pass same-sex marriage in New York after identifying a coalition of Republicans who are willing to vote their conscience. "Marriage equality changed life for people," Governor Cuomo later said. "It provided a level of acceptance for millions of people and their families."

September 20, 2011. "Don't Ask, Don't Tell" is repealed.

September 30, 2011. Congressman Jared Polis (D-Colorado) becomes first openly gay member of Congress to become a parent.

2012. Leaders of the DNC agree to include same-sex marriage and the repeal of DOMA on the party platform for 2012.

February 13, 2012. Governor Christine Gregoire signs the Freedom to Marry Act into law, making Washington the first state to repeal its own Defense of Marriage Act.

May 9, 2012. President Obama publicly endorses marriage equality.

July 7, 2012. Barney Frank becomes the first sitting congressman to enter into a same-sex marriage with partner James Ready.

November 6, 2012. Maine and Maryland legalize gay marriage by popular vote; Minnesota fails to pass a permanent amendment banning gay marriage; and Washington voters reject a referendum to overturn marriage equality—marking the first time the issue has won at the ballot box.

December 2012. The Supreme Court agrees to hear two separate cases regarding gay marriage.

February 25, 2013. Dozens of prominent Republicans, including influential businesswoman Meg Whitman and former Utah governor and ambassador to China Jon Huntsman Jr., sign an amicus brief arguing that gay people have a constitutional right to marry.

June 26, 2013. A great day for civil rights: the Supreme Court, in two 5–4 decisions with different compositions of justices, rules in support of gay marriage. In the DOMA case—*US v. Windsor*—the law barring the federal government from recognizing same-sex marriages legalized by individual states is deemed unconstitutional. A second case lets stand a ruling that found California's 2008 Proposition 8—a voter initiative banning gay marriages—to be illegal.

MARRIAGE EQUALITY RESOURCE GUIDE

The story of marriage equality begins with near-total acceptance of second-class status for a large swath of Americans—and ends with an overwhelming sense of inevitability that all people are entitled to access to the benefits of marriage. That enormous change—as well as the continuing manifestation of this "sure thing"—is the result of thousands of individuals acting in small ways to change their own perspective, that of their communities, and ultimately lawmakers' views, bills, and votes.

So, what can we do to continue the work celebrated in this volume? Each day there are countless opportunities to interrupt the status quo and shape the world so that it more closely hews to the ideals on which this nation was founded. To name a few:

- You can write your representatives on the state and federal level and let them know you support equal marriage and want representatives in office who share those values. If your elected officials already support marriage equality, send them a thank you note—in many states, it's still a brave position to take and kind words are always good for courage.
- Scour your local paper for stories relating to marriage rights and write a letter to the editor in response. It gives you a chance to voice your

opinion to a broad audience—and emboldens others to do the same.

- You can get involved with or donate to any of the organizations below, all of which have wonderful human rights agendas that include marriage equality.

American Civil Liberties Union

In addition to being "our nation's guardian of liberty, working daily in courts, legislatures, and communities to defend and preserve the individual rights and liberties that the Constitution and laws of the United States guarantee everyone," the ACLU sued the federal government on behalf of Edith Windsor to overturn the Defense of Marriage Act in 2013. Every state and Puerto Rico has its own affiliate, and the national organization can be reached at:

125 Broad Street, 18th Floor
New York, NY 10004
Phone: 212-549-2500
www.aclu.org

Audre Lorde Project

"There is no such thing as a single-issue struggle because we do not live single-issue lives." So said the great lesbian poet warrior who is the namesake of this organization. Her words embellish millions of e-mails from idealists around the world, and this organization, devoted to her memory, is explicitly antisexist and recognizes the full diversity of gay communities of color.

Manhattan:
147 West 24th Street, 3rd Floor
New York, NY 10011
Phone: 212-463-0342

Brooklyn:
85 South Oxford Street
Brooklyn, NY 11217
Phone: 718-596-0342
www.alp.org

BiNet USA

As the foremost umbrella organization representing bisexual, pansexual, and fluid communities, BiNet supports marriage equality, immigration reform to support queer families and avoid needless separation, and the right to adopt, foster, and have child custody.

4201 Wilson Boulevard, #110-311
Arlington, VA 22203
Phone: 1-800-585-9368
www.binetusa.org

Family Equality Council

The Family Equality Council "is committed to achieving family equality for all types of families" and to making marriage an option for any couple who desires that right.

Washington, DC:
1050 17th Street NW, Suite 600
Washington, DC 20036

Boston:
41 Winter Street, 3rd Floor
Boston, MA 02108
Phone: 617-502-8700
Fax: 617-502-8701
www.familyequality.org

Freedom to Marry
This civil rights campaign has partnered "with individuals and organizations across the country to end the exclusion of same-sex couples from marriage and the protections, responsibilities, and commitment that marriage brings" since 2003. Evan Wolfson, a key figure in the struggle for marriage equality, is the founder.

New York City:
155 West 19th Street, 2nd Floor
New York, NY 10011
Phone: 212-851-8418
Fax: 646-375-2069

Washington, DC:
2120 L Street NW, Suite 850
Washington, DC 20037
Phone: 202-223-0732
Fax: 202-223-0082
www.freedomtomarry.org

Gay and Lesbian Advocates and Defenders
According to GLAD's website, "Whether it's marriage for same-sex couples, nondiscrimination policies for

transgender people in the workplace, or protections for people with HIV, GLAD doesn't shrink from tough issues. And we don't compromise on our belief that every citizen deserves full equality under the law—without exception."

30 Winter Street, Suite 800
Boston, MA 02108
Phone: 617-426-1350
www.glad.org

Human Rights Campaign

According to HRC's website, "We are mothers and fathers, brothers and sisters. We are friends and neighbors and colleagues. We are lesbian, gay, bisexual, transgender, and straight. We believe every American has the right to marry the person they love."

1640 Rhode Island Avenue NW
Washington, DC 20036
Phone: 202-628-4160
Fax: 202-347-5323
www.hrc.org

International Gay and Lesbian Human Rights Commission

This pioneering international activist organization was founded in 1990 by Julie Dorf, who believes that "all people, regardless of their sexual orientation, gender identity, or HIV status" deserve human rights.

80 Maiden Lane, Suite 1505
New York, NY 10038

Phone: 212-430-6054
Fax: 212-430-6060
www.iglhrc.org

Lambda Legal

From winning the freedom to marry to defending domestic partnership benefits and securing parent-child relationships, Lambda Legal protects same-sex couples and their families through a broad range of litigation, education, and advocacy strategies.

120 Wall Street, 19th Floor
New York, NY 10005
Phone: 212-809-8585
Fax: 212-809-0055
www.lambdalegal.org

Log Cabin Republicans

Gay Republicans need organizations too. According to Executive Director Gregory T. Angelo, "Log Cabin Republicans will continue to be on the front lines to take the conservative case for marriage to Republicans across the nation."

1090 Vermont Avenue NW, Suite 850
Washington, DC 20005
Phone: 202-420-7873
www.logcabin.org

Marriage Equality

Marriage Equality USA (MEUSA) is the nation's oldest and largest grassroots, volunteer-driven organization dedicated solely to securing the right for all Americans to enter into legally recognized civil marriages.

PO Box 121, Old Chelsea Station
New York, NY 10113
Phone: 347-913-6369
Fax: 347-479-1700
www.marriageequality.org

National Gay and Lesbian Task Force
NGLTF believes that the respect, many rights, and protections marriage provides are essential to the well-being of all families. Since the 1970s, NGLTF has worked to lobby, change our culture, and train activists, responding to the most pressing needs of the gay community.

Washington, DC:
1325 Massachusetts Avenue NW, Suite 600
Washington, DC 20005
Phone: 202-393-5177
Fax: 202-393-2241

New York City:
80 Maiden Lane, Suite 1504
New York, NY 10038
Phone: 212-604-9830
Fax: 212-604-9831

Cambridge, MA:
1151 Massachusetts Avenue
Cambridge, MA 02138

Phone: 617-492-6393
Fax: 617-492-0175

Miami, FL:
801 Arthur Godfrey Road, Suite 402
Miami Beach, FL 33140
Phone: 305-571-1924
Fax: 305-571-7298

Minneapolis, MN:
122 West Franklin Avenue, Suite 210
Minneapolis, MN 55404
Phone: 612-821-4397
Fax: 612-821-4397
www.ngltf.org